# The Judge Talks Politics

## An Insider's View on Law and Government

*Francis Donovan*

iUniverse, Inc.
New York   Bloomington

# The Judge Talks Politics

## An Insider's View on Law and Government

iUniverse books may be ordered through booksellers or by contacting:

iUniverse
1663 Liberty Drive
Bloomington, IN 47403
www.iuniverse.com
1-800-Authors (1-800-288-4677)

ISBN: 978-0-595-42941-7 (pbk)
ISBN: 978-1-4401-0004-8 (cloth)
ISBN: 978-0-595-87283-1 (ebk)

Printed in the United States of America

This book is owned by:

Francis J. Donovan

14 Field Avenue

Hicksville, NY 11801

Office: 90 Newbridge Road

Hicksville, NY 11801

Phone: (516) 938-1717

E-mail: Fdonova1@optonline.net

# Contents

# CHAPTER ONE

## *Margiotta v. Donovan*

More times than I can remember, I have asked myself, "Do we really need another book on politics?" The witty former mayor of the city of New York, Ed Koch; the brilliant and philosophical former governor of the state of New York, Mario Cuomo; and other major political personalities have favored us with their wit and wisdom. Why compete with such "heavyweights"? Why bother to undertake such a job?

I will make this attempt for two reasons:

1. For my own peace of mind, I must get it out of my head and put it on paper.

2. None of the books I have read give the reader any insight into or understanding of the mechanics of politics.

The political bosses, managers, public relations persons, and the like know the rules, the targets, and how to reach them, but these experts are loath to reveal their secrets. Why share the secrets, the knowledge that gives them the advantage over the less informed? For what it is worth, I will tell my story. It is personal. It is short. It is simple. It may open some eyes. It begins with a naïve, unemployed young lawyer who developed legal and political skills until he attracted the anger of the powerful political Boss of the dominant political party on Long Island. In an unprecedented battle, he was the surprising victor against the Boss of the Republican Party in the county of Nassau and the most powerful Republican leader in New York State.

There is a case reported in volume 29 on page 725 of the *Official Reports of Court of Appeals of the State of New York*, 2nd Edition, under the title "In the Matter of Donovan v. Tese." It would have been more accurately entitled "Margiotta v. Donovan." I am the "Donovan," plaintiff in that case. Defendant Tese, a minor official in the town of Oyster Bay, New York, was merely a stand-in for the Republican Party Boss, Joseph Margiotta (hereinafter sometimes referred to as "Boss"). It was a political fight that pitted myself, a lower court judge, against the boss of my political party. It was to be a campaign waged in courts and the public forum on an issue never before litigated in New York State.

Margiotta was at the height of his power. He was arrogant and unchallenged and controlled a vast army of Republican community leaders, public employees, contractors, and their friends and families. Using bipartisan judgeships, patronage, and deals, he had neutralized the opposing Democratic Party. What sparked the fight was a deal Margiotta had made with the Democratic Party. It was designed to destroy the power of a small third party, the Conservative Party. The deal would destroy the ability of the Conservatives to swing elections by endorsing major party candidates. The bipartisan agreement was called "The Cross-Endorsement Ban." Margiotta had obtained the support of the two local newspapers, *Newsday* and the *Long Island Press*, for enforcement of the Ban. The thing that bound these parties together in support of the Ban was their common interest in eliminating the Conservative Party as a player in local elections.

The agreement read:

I support the principles and precepts of the Republican Party. As inducement for the support of the County Committee of the Republican Party, I hereby agree that I shall not accept the designation or nomination of another political party or independent organization or political body. I am also aware of, and understand, the sanctions which may be invoked by the Republican Party or another political party or independent organization or political group.

I had served two terms as a District Court judge. In accordance with the existing practice of the major parties, I and all other sitting judges had received the nominations of both the Republican and Democrat Parties. I had also received the nomination of the Conservative Party. Boss Margiotta demanded that I reject the Conservative nomination. All I had to do was sign a rejection form and file it with the Board of Elections. I was guaranteed election as the candidate of both major parties. Every other judicial candidate signed the Ban. Why should I refuse? The Ban had been approved by the courts in a case brought by Lewis Yevoli, a Democratic candidate for town councilman from the town of Oyster Bay. Why did I rebel?

Apparently neither the Boss nor any of his advisors had considered the Ban in the light of the Canons of Judicial Ethics. That issue had not been involved in the Yevoli case. One did not have to be a legal scholar or do extensive research to see the conflict between the Canons of Judicial Ethics and a judge's signing a political agreement such as the Cross-Endorsement Ban. To pose the question is to compel the answer. The Canons of Judicial Ethics forbade any judge from engaging in partisan political activity. The question presented to every judge by the Cross-Endorsement Ban was, "Do I refuse to obey the Boss and prejudice my position or do I go along?" No judge could have pled innocent to a charge of ethical violation where the issue was so clear. In framing the issue, I wrote a formal legal memorandum, and I sent that memorandum to Judge Farley, who was then the chief judge in Nassau County. The issue was discussed in private conversations among judges, lawyers, and politicians. This was an issue where there should have been no doubt in anyone's mind. If a judge becomes a party to an agreement negotiated by two political parties and designed to accomplish a partisan political objective, how could he be doing anything other than "engaging in partisan political activity"? Perhaps the Boss did not see it, or more likely, in his arrogance, he brushed it aside. At any rate, I saw the problem and refused to reject the Conservative nomination and refused to sign the Ban.

I was the only judge, or judicial candidate, to refuse to sign the Ban. Why was I alone in defying the Ban? It seemed that others would have spoken out against this assault on the judiciary. Perhaps the Judicial Conference of the state of New York, the State or County Bar Association, the chief administrative judge of Nassau County, or some other member of the judiciary might speak out? So powerful were the Boss and his political machine that not a single voice was raised. Despite the fact that for a judge to sign that pledge was a clear and flagrant violation of the Canons of Judicial Ethics, no judge, no judicial candidate, no appellate judge, and no Bar Association uttered a word. All were silent. I stood alone, isolated, and cut off from both Republican and Democrat parties. The Boss was ready to attack. The fight was on. It was a fight that could have been avoided. If we want to number the Boss's tactical errors, this was number one. He was launching a major public contest over a minor political office.

In a similar case some years before, the most astute of political leaders, J. Russell Sprague, former Nassau county executive and county Republican leader, had quashed a town leader's plan to eliminate a District Court judge. As Sprague's primary legal advisor, I was present at the conference between Sprague and that judge's town leader. Under the party rules, a town leader determines all patronage and approves all candidates for public office from his town. The judge who had aroused the ire of his town leader was Albert

Moore from the town of North Hempstead. Norman Penny, political leader of that town, told Sprague that he did not want to have Moore nominated for re-election.

Sprague, with his usual style of seeming to acquiesce with the position of his adversary, said, "Norm, he's your judge. If you want to dump him, that is your right, but be prepared to explain to the public why you are throwing out a judge with a good reputation and whom you have twice supported for that office."

Judge Moore was re-nominated and re-elected.

Margiotta was no Sprague. He was a bully, intoxicated with power. A former collegiate football player, he was a big, stocky, athletic type. By nature, relying on power, he would be prone to attack. He was reared in a middle-class suburb on Long Island. He had come up through the ranks of the Republican Party through local party work leading to nomination and election to the New York State Legislature. He learned how to succeed and how to exercise control in the political arena. Obey the leader. Pay your dues on the way up. When you are "up," hold your position by making deals and dispensing patronage. We would not have expected the Boss to make tactical blunders in his campaign to destroy me. It would have appeared that I was no match for a political giant such as Margiotta backed by his army of political office holders and operatives.

By contrast to the Boss, I am diminutive in stature. In my youth I too was athletic, but lacking bulk and height, I had to rely on speed and maneuverability. In my prime I stood five feet two inches tall and weighed 115 pounds. My family was a poor family that endured all the hardship common to the poor. We survived without any public assistance. It was a hard life, but we emerged as resourceful people who learned to "do without." I attended college and law school without the money required to obtain such an education. I attended prep school and college on scholarships and worked after school during college. The law school scholarship was earned by being first in my class each year.

I graduated from St. John's Law School as a Doctor of Laws with the distinction "Summa Cum Laude." Despite my scholastic achievements, I was under the twin handicaps of coming from a poor family and graduating from a law school that, at that time, was not a recruiting ground for major New York law firms. Throughout my life, I had fought many battles, usually as an underdog defying the powerful. In short, if challenged, I could give one trouble. Margiotta was not the first powerful person with whom I had come into conflict. I never sought such battles, but the adversary never cowed me. I neither sought a battle with the Boss nor expected one.

The District Court judgeship was a minor political position. It was not important enough to become a bone of contention. However, I became apprehensive when I received a phone call from Appellate Division Judge Marcus Christ. Christ had been county attorney prior to his ascension to the bench. He had hired me as a deputy county attorney in that office. Apparently he had become aware of an impending conflict between the Boss and me. Judge Christ told me to be careful when I met Margiotta and to avoid making him angry. He also said that Margiotta would be foolish to attack a sitting judge with a good reputation.

While I hoped to avoid a fight, I had prepared a defense. I had composed a short legal memorandum demonstrating the conflict between the Ban and the Canons of Judicial Ethics. Prior to meeting with Margiotta, I sent copies of that memorandum to Supreme Court Judge Farley, the Chief Administrative Judge in Nassau County, and the New York State Judicial Conference. As events unraveled, Margiotta did get angry, and the battle was joined. Before confronting me, Margiotta began to use his contacts to get key people to contact me and urge me to change my mind.

First there was a call from Judge Farley asking me to meet him. Farley knew me well. We had been friends for over twenty-five years. Years earlier, when Farley was a young county judge and I was Sprague's chief legal advisor, Sprague asked my advice on one of Farley's cases. The case involved the sale of a house for unpaid taxes. Apparently the case had been discussed between Farley and Sprague, and Sprague wanted a decision in favor of the homeowner. I agreed with Sprague's decision. Apparently Farley had difficulty in writing the opinion. Sprague asked me to write the opinion for Farley. I wrote an opinion, and Farley issued the opinion as his own.

As an aside, you may not be aware that a person, or a lawyer, will go to a political leader for help. Further, it is not uncommon for a political leader to speak to a judge on a pending matter. Nor is it uncommon for an unknown to write an opinion and a judge to issue that opinion as his own. There was nothing immoral in this scenario. Sprague did not tell me what to write. He asked for my opinion. I was the county's tax expert. My opinion was based on a study of the applicable law. The decision was correct and stood up on appeal. With apology for the digression, let us return to an older Farley. He had risen to the position of Chief Judge, presiding over all of the judges in the county. Neither age nor elevation had changed him. At our conference, Farley never said a word about the issue. All he could offer was a cowardly comment, "When you see Joe (Margiotta), be sure to tell him that I had nothing to do with this."

Next came a surprise phone call from an attorney on the staff of the New York State Judicial Conference. Here again one would have expected an independent consideration of the ethical issue. Not so. The attorney's mission was obviously intended to have me back off the issue. He too did not discuss the issue. His advice was something less than we would have expected from a person in such a position.

His advice was, "We think that you can sign the agreement since it was left open in the Yevoli case."

Any knowledgeable lawyer would have understood that where an issue is neither raised nor discussed in a case, the decision in that case is irrelevant when that issue is raised in a later case. Clearly he was evading the issue and offering me a way to back off.

Next came a visit to my home by attorney Peter Affatato. Peter was a prominent trial lawyer and a friend of mine for many years. He was well connected in legal and political circles. I told Peter that after having publicly declared that signing the Ban was a breach of ethics, I could not change my mind. Peter's visit was followed by a phone call from another old friend, Bill Meisser. Bill had been Commissioner of Elections during my tenure as deputy county attorney. His department was one of those that came under my jurisdiction. I had written many legal opinions for him and successfully handled every election litigation that arose during his time. Bill had been retired for a number of years. As a prelude, Bill began to tell me about the board's problems in printing ballots and setting up elections. He then came to the point of my decision on the Ban. I told Bill what I had told to Affatato: even if I wanted to, I could not sign a Ban that I had clearly and forcefully denounced as a breach of ethics.

All else having failed, confident of his power, the Boss summoned me to a "conference" at the Republican Headquarters in Hempstead. Seated on a dais, very much like an appellate court, were my "judges," the three leaders, County Leader Margiotta, Town Leader Roncallo, and Village Leader Trotta. I was seated below them, much as a defendant in a criminal court. The staging was obviously contrived to intimidate me.

The Boss opened by saying, "All judges expect to be promoted."

I replied, "I never expect to be promoted. Shall I tell you why?"

The Boss was well aware of the problems created by my having repulsed efforts by political leaders to influence my judicial conduct. He did not want to hear an answer to his statement.

Oyster Bay's town leader, Angelo Roncallo, asked to see a copy of the memorandum I had circulated showing the conflict between the pledge and the Canons of Judicial Ethics. Roncallo read the memorandum and said he did not want a primary contest in his town "with the Irish fighting the Italians." However, the Boss was not to be dissuaded. He then uttered a threat with an apologetic tone saying, "The Democratic leader will think I have reneged on him if I don't do anything."

I replied, "You know that I will defend myself."

At that the meeting ended. In the light of Roncallo's comment, I did not expect a primary fight. I was wrong. The Boss was angry, and his attack was immediate and public. He set out to destroy me, to hold me out as an object lesson as what would happen to anyone who did not obey party discipline. Party discipline, in the Boss's vocabulary, meant "my orders." It was the Boss against an insubordinate little judge. The Boss would make an example of this little judge. He would demonstrate his control over the judiciary. The Boss pulled no punches. His opening salvo was a press release in which he said, "It's Donovan and his family and friends against the organization."

The Boss rammed through the County Committee a resolution that I should not only be driven from office but that I should also never again hold public office. He then set out to remove me from the Republican ballot by a primary election "write-in" campaign.

The opening salvo by Margiotta defined the contest. The organization was the Republican Committee with its thousands of neighborhood captains, town and county employees, and their families. Opposed was myself with the minor party Conservatives, my family, and "friends." The district in which the primary would be held was comprised of the small city of Glen Cove and the large town of Oyster Bay. A primary election is an intraparty affair and draws a small vote. Since no nominating petition had been filed by either the Republican or Democratic parties in opposition, I could only have been challenged by a write-in vote. Surprisingly, the Democrats did not mount a write-in campaign. This meant that I would appear on the ballot in the general election as the Democratic and Conservative Party candidate, but there would be a contest for the Republican nomination between the Boss's candidate, Tese and myself. Without an organization, I could not mount a townwide campaign. I had been active in religious, fraternal, and civic associations in my hometown, the hamlet of Hicksville. I had served as president of the Hicksville Republican Club. I decided to draw on that reservoir and bring out every Republican voter in Hicksville. If I could bring out the Hicksville voters en masse, they might be enough to beat a low turnout in the rest of the town.

In such a campaign, I would need maps of the town and lists of voters with their enrollment and addresses for the campaign workers. These had to be obtained from the County Board of Elections. Strangely, without any request from me, or any message from anybody, an unidentified messenger delivered a package containing maps of the district and lists of voters to my house. I had no trouble identifying that messenger. He had to be a person with access to the records of the Board of Elections. He had to be a person with knowledge of what was needed in election campaigns. He had to be a person with a special interest in my success. He had to be a "friend." The only person with all those qualifications was James Moore, a Democratic committeeman from the village of Bayville in the town of Oyster Bay. James Moore was the chief clerk of the Board of Elections. That board was exclusively staffed with political workers from the two major parties. It differed from other county departments in that the employees took no examinations to qualify for their jobs. Their sole qualification was political work for one of those two parties. The board was headed by two chairpersons, one from the Republican Party and one from the Democratic Party. Employees were similarly divided with an equal number from each party. However, in day-to-day operations, Jimmy Moore was "the Board of Elections." He had worked there for years. He knew where everything was and supervised all of the board's operations. In that capacity, Jimmy had worked with me for many years. During the ten years I had been counsel to the Board, he and I had become close friends. The Boss did not know about this "friend." My "friends" were operating ...

To staff my campaign, I called "friends" in Hicksville to set up a meeting of volunteers. About one hundred men answered the call. I knew personally almost every one of them. The first item of business was to select a chairperson for the campaign committee. Only one man volunteered for that job. He was a newcomer, and I did not know him. He told me that he had worked on Republican campaigns in Queens, an adjoining county. Since he was the only volunteer who had any experience in election campaigning, he was appointed and given the maps of the area and lists of the voters. The plan was to assign the men to particular election districts and have each of them contact the voters in a particular district. That appointment proved to be an error. On the day of the primary election, not a single Hicksville voter was contacted. My chairman never contacted a single volunteer. He took the maps and lists and disappeared. The sabotage was successful, and the saboteur was rewarded. He was later appointed law secretary to Justice McCaffrey, one of the Republican Supreme Court Judges.

The Boss's candidate, Carmel Tese, was a town employee whose primary qualification was his name. In a write-in campaign, ballots are often declared invalid because of misspelled names, so a four-letter name is ideal for a candidate. It eliminates the problem of spelling. Tese's second qualification was his nationality. The majority of Republican voters in Glen Cove and Oyster Bay were Italian. Aided by my chairman's sabotage and the strength of the Republican machine, Tese won the primary by a margin of one thousand votes. Had my one hundred men been contacted for work in getting out the vote in Hicksville, I might have won. But this was not the end of the contest. Tese was not yet the Republican candidate to oppose me.

Calling on my experience as an elections litigator, I filed a court challenge to the result of the primary election. In my petition to the court, I made a routine demand for a recount of the ballots, but added a novel challenge, demanding that Tese be disqualified on the ground that his victory was the product of a conspiracy by two lawyers, Tese and Margiotta, to compel a judge to violate the Canons of Judicial Ethics. Attentive to the adage that says, "The man who represents himself in litigation has a fool for a lawyer," I prepared all the papers but had a young lawyer, son of another "friend," Charlie Schutzman, appear in court. The court dismissed my petition on both counts without making any comment on the ethics issue. I immediately appealed to the Appellate Division of the Supreme Court.

Election litigations are unique in the speed with which they must proceed and the summary nature of the deliberations. Two days after the dismissal of my petition by the lower court, my case was called for argument in the Appellate Court. It was heard en Banc. The court did not convene in the large courtroom where cases are regularly heard. It convened in a conference room where the judges sat on one side of a large table and the lawyers and parties sat on the opposite side. This informality can be an advantage or disadvantage depending on the style of the attorney. Young Schutzman began his argument, and the Court interrupted, indicating it might send the case back to the lower court because the judge in that court had not made findings-of-fact in his decision. Knowing that I could not win on a recount and knowing that I would need the permission of the Appellate Division to appeal to the Court of Appeals, I realized that young Schutzman was not the lawyer for this case.

I stood up and asked to be allowed to represent myself. My request was granted. Using an unorthodox approach, I presented a deal I felt might appeal to the judges' sense of fair play. I told them that I would waive my right to a recount of the ballots if they would give me permission to appeal to the Court of Appeals on the ethics issue. The gambit worked. The Appellate Division affirmed the dismissal of my petition but gave me permission to appeal to the Court of Appeals. For the student of political science, there is a small lesson to be learned about judges. Judges are not selected based on legal scholarship. They do not qualify by competitive examinations. Without disparaging any of them, we must remember that they worked their way up a political ladder. They accepted the rules and limitations of the system. They are unlikely to make any drastic changes. They are not prone to nullifying elections. At the same time, most of them have an innate tendency to be fair. In any case, the lawyer must read the judge. In my case, the appeal court could have sent the case back to the court below to have that court amend its decision. This would have been fatal since my time to get a final decision would have expired. (In a later chapter discussing the case of Gore against Bush, the critical effect of time limit will be illustrated.)

While the courtroom and the decorum and solemnity of the judges and attorneys tends to convey the impression that the court reaches its decisions based on a scholarly review of precedents and solemn debate. I was brief. I was different. I caught their attention with my novel approach. On we went to the Court of Appeals.

Despite their robes and the somber atmosphere of the court, its members are the product of a practical political process. They are sharp and incisive and can be expected to be particularly so in election cases. The argument in the Court of Appeals would have to be tailored to appeal to the attitude of such judges. It would have to be made up on the spot as the mood of the court might require. It could not be constructed on legal precedent or some academic legal theory. The case was without precedent. Never before had any court been asked to nullify an election because of ethical violation.

My argument began in a simple but formal style. It quickly changed to a sharp exchange between the court and me. Shortly into the oral argument, Judge Scileppi, challenged me. Scileppi had been very active in Queens County politics. He was prominent in the Elks organization. He got around and enjoyed broad popularity. He got to the Court of Appeals in an election where he had defeated my political mentor, Marcus Christ, though the latter was clearly superior in qualifications. Scileppi was the ultimate city politician. Mindful of how judges were made, he was clearly unsympathetic to what appeared to him to be an ungrateful guy turning on those who made him. Scileppi asked, "Wasn't it a political act when you accepted the Conservative endorsement?"

It was apparent to me that Scileppi had not studied the record and did not know the election law. This was no longer a matter of discussion between judge and advocate. Scileppi was looking for a fight. He was going to expose me for what I was, a guy turning on those who made him. This was going to be "man-to-man" combat.

I took off the gloves and replied, "Your Honor, if you will check the record, you will find that I never accepted the Conservative endorsement. I stood silent. The Election Law requires that a candidate nominated by a party other than his own must file a written acceptance of that nomination if he is to become a candidate of that other party. However, judges are exempted from that requirement. The judge can stand silent and he will be the nominee of that party."

That ended Scileppi's challenge.

I now had the attention of the court. It was now my time to make a challenge. Well aware that the court was reluctant to nullify the election and aroused by Scileppi's challenge, I challenged the court with an argument that went to their ethical and moral sense. I closed my argument with an emotional plea, "I come from Brooklyn where we played under peculiar conditions. We often had special ground rules for the game. I can play by any rules that you want. I can follow the dictate of the Canons of Judicial Ethics or I can obey the county political leader. Tell me which way I must go and I will do it!"

My unorthodox behavior got results. The court affirmed the dismissal of my petition but answered the ethical question saying:

Political organization leaders ought not exact a promise of party loyalty from candidates for political office as a condition of support, and such candidates should not make these promises in exchange for support.

I had not knocked Tese out, but I had what I needed. The state's highest court said that the Boss's conduct and that of those who cravenly submitted to his order had violated the Canons of Judicial ethics. The court had framed the campaign issue. The issue was judicial ethics. Battle was joined.

Before going into the campaign you may ask: What can be learned from the matter discussed in the preceding chapter? Why did Donovan write it? There are two reasons for my tale. One is personal and the other educational. First is my pride in having succeeded in using a judicial proceeding to frame a campaign issue. Second is to give the reader a graphic illustration of the interaction of judges and politicians. The tools that I used in this litigation were not learned in law school. They were acquired in the rough-and-tumble life in Brooklyn, sports, fistfights, and work in the Wallabout Market. The Wallabout was a huge outdoor market where Long Island's farmers trucked in their produce. I had worked there as a "carrier." A carrier loaded and unloaded the trucks and carried the huge baskets and sacks that were used to transport the produce. It was a rough, competitive environment where you fought to survive.

The judicial contest is called "litigation." The word "litigation" is derived from the Latin word *litis* meaning "contest or fight." One should prepare for litigation as for any fight. You must analyze the strengths and weaknesses of yourself and your opponent. You should also learn something about the referee, or judge, and his bias. In my litigation, Margiotta had a huge political advantage. The judges had grown up in the political arena. They would be inclined to view the case through the eyes of a political leader such as the Boss. Despite that bias, most judges have an innate sense of fair play. Both biases would be in play. My appeal had to be to their sense of fair play. The political bias came to the surface in the colloquy between Judge Scillepi, the most politically oriented of judges, and myself. My challenge to the court placed them in a dilemma. I was willing to play by the Boss's rules or the ethical rules. Would the judges answer, in a public courtroom, "Obey the Boss," or would they say, "Obey the ethical rules"? They went for the ethics, another little motivation that operated on the judges. They liked the fight. They liked the fighter. Their sporting instinct and their sense of fair play weighed in to give me the affirmation of my ethical stance.

# CHAPTER TWO

## *Organizing the Campaign*

Before advancing to the campaign, we might pause to find out why the Democrats did not conduct a write-in to purge me from their ballot. I was a conservative Republican. For those who like to define all issues and all candidates as either liberal or conservative, I should have been anathema to the Democratic organization. Again, my "friends" were operating. There was a small group of conservative Democrats still active in the organization. A leader in that group was a friend of mine named George O'Haire. George was Democratic leader of Hicksville. However that group alone could never have held back the Democratic organization. A more important figure was Judge Beatrice Burstein. Judge Burstein had been a thorn in the side of the Republican Party for years. She would have been categorized as a liberal Democrat. When she succeeded in becoming a District Court judge, she was the only Democrat in a court that had been exclusively staffed by Republicans from its inception. While Judge Burstein was a very intelligent woman, her experience in trials was limited. She had problems adjusting to her new job and no one was giving her much help or attention. I gave her a few tips on the art of judging and gave her moral support. As time went on, we developed respect for each other despite our different political philosophies. One day, while going to lunch, we met. Judge Burstein was on her way to appear on a radio program. She asked me if I would like to join her on the program. I accepted the invitation. As the program began, Judge Burstein introduced me and said, "Since becoming judges, I have become more conservative, and Judge Donovan has become more liberal."

That sentence reveals much about her character. Neither she nor I were blindly liberal nor blindly conservative. We could differentiate between ethical and unethical.

When the fight between me and the Boss became known, Judge Burstein called me and told me to call her husband, partner in a major New York City law firm, and to call her publicity agent, Marcia Abramson. As a silent ally and a leading figure in the Democratic Party, she very quietly moved to protect me from a loss of the Democratic nomination. Without that Democratic line on the ballot, I could not possibly have hoped to win, and I would have withdrawn from the contest.

As the political battle opened, there was a gross mismatch. The experts gave me little chance of winning. The sides matched up with the Boss possessing overwhelming manpower and finances. He had access to the huge Republican treasury and the "organization" that embraced hordes of precinct workers and employees. He also had the support of the two local newspapers, *Newsday* and *Long Island Press*. I had to finance my own campaign. I had no fundraisers and no campaign committee. I was not about to impoverish my family by risking my savings on a game where the odds were solidly against me My campaign cost $1,500, which was paid by myself. Such an impoverished campaign had to be waged by friends on the cheap. There were no funds for advertising or to pay for campaign offices or staff. I had a handful of workers from the Conservative Party, and in the words of the Boss, my "friends and family." I had no organization, but I had many workers. There were Democrats such as Judge Burstein, Jimmy Moore, and George O'Haire working unannounced and anonymous. I had lawyers such as my old classmate Bill Hanrahan and my old friend Charles Schutzman contacting fellow lawyers and friends. I still had that hundred men who would have worked on my primary campaign and as many women in Hicksville contacting families, friends, and neighbors in my behalf. I did not have the huge army that the Boss put into the field, but my army was loyal, devoted, and inspired. The Boss's army was under duress and given the chance, many would desert him.

Although I appeared on the Democratic line on the ballot, I was not the candidate of that party. The Democratic county chairman publicly declared that the Democrat Party would give me neither support nor money nor workers. In the light of that announcement and my identification with the Conservative Party, I would have a special problem in holding core Democrats. Experience in prior local campaigns demonstrated that a Democratic candidate with Conservative endorsement would suffer attrition on the Democratic line. I tried to minimize that exposure by attending no Democratic functions and sending no letters to Democratic voters. By attracting no attention, I hoped to avoid becoming a target for the straight-line Democratic voter. The game plan was to ignore them while trying to pick off Republicans and attract Independents.

The district in which I was to run had some large communities and some small ones. I decided to leave out the small communities and restrict my effort to the large communities, namely the city of Glen Cove, the villages of Farmingdale, Massapequa, and Syosset. Relying on my years of community activity in my home village, Hicksville, I planned no special effort there. I prepared for battle as one would prepare a military campaign. I was vastly outnumbered and grossly inferior in arms and ammunition. The fundamental plan in any military battle is to conserve your forces and to inflict losses on your adversary. In a political battle, you must keep your core voters intact while attracting independents and capturing, or picking off, some of your adversary's core voters. If your core is vastly superior to your adversary's, the emphasis is on playing to, and preserving, your core. The posture is geared to defense. If you are the underdog, your emphasis must be on attracting independents and picking off votes from your adversary's core. The posture is geared to attack.

From a statistical point of view, I faced an uphill battle. The registration records of the Nassau Board of Elections for the Judicial District comprising the town of Oyster Bay and city of Glen Cove showed the following numbers:

Republican: 76,635

Democrat: 56,177

Conservative: 3,371

If I held the Democratic core and the Conservative core, I would have 59,548 votes to Tese's Republican core of 76,635 votes. If every registered voter voted his or her line, I would lose by 17, 087 votes. To make up that deficit, I would have to hold every Democratic vote and draw 17,087 additional votes from elsewhere, namely Independents and Republicans. Many Independents restrict their voting to presidential or gubernatorial elections. There was little hope of having any great number of them vote in this off-year local election. The deficit would increase if some Democrats were picked off. This would be expected since Cristenfeld, the Democratic County Chairman, had publicly declared that the Democratic Party would give me no support, monetary or otherwise. Other Democrats, seeing the Conservative label on me, would either skip my name or vote for a liberal. However, that gap would be lessened if I could pick off Republicans. Every Republican that I captured would count twice. It would be minus one for the Republican tally and plus one for the Democratic tally. If nine thousand Republican voters could be turned to me, that would subtract nine thousand from Tese, making the total eighteen thousand votes needed to close the gap. Clearly the major effort had to be directed to picking off registered Republicans.

The attack on the Boss's core was launched from several directions. Special groups that usually supported Republican candidates such as policemen, lawyers, and ethnic groups were targeted. Large, predominantly Republican communities were targeted. Police and lawyers got special attention. They knew and appreciated my record for judicial independence and exceptional knowledge of the law. They would understand the vice of a partisan judiciary and have a sporting respect for a fighter. Policemen were numerous in Nassau County. They favored that county because it had the suburban character they wanted for their families and was convenient to their work in New York City. The town of Oyster Bay was home to New York City police, Parkway police, New York City transit police, as well as Nassau County police. It was not necessary for me to do much in the campaign for police. I had strong ties to those voters. I had been closely associated with both the Nassau Police Emerald Society and Nassau Police Steuben Society in their formative days. I spoke—and sometimes sang—at their dinners. I marched with them in parades and mingled with them at picnics. They were "friends" who needed no prodding to get into the campaign. That became clear at a meeting called by Frank Bolz, head of the New York State Police Steuben Society and a nationally recognized hostage negotiator. Bolz called a meeting for the leaders of the Steubens and me. At that meeting, I told the Steubens that perhaps they should not get involved because Margiotta might take it out on them by blocking legislation in which they had an interest. Bolz quickly responded, "I think we can take care of ourselves!" I took this to mean that I should let the police handle their own campaign and I did.

Another prong of the campaign targeted lawyers. Bill Hanrahan, a law school classmate of mine, spearheaded that campaign. He spoke to lawyers at the courts and gave them literature. He also restarted me and drove me on at a time when I thought of letting go because I was tired and the strain was too wearing. I was amazed at the support from lawyers. Many of them had suffered losses in my court and they got no special treatment. What they did get was fair treatment, and they knew that I did my best to find the right decision. Perhaps it is a result of their training and experience, but many lawyers have a sporting attitude. They enjoy a contest. They may exult in a win but can accept a loss with grace. Many became involved and distributed my literature to their clients. These were all "friends" that the Boss had not counted.

A third prong of the campaign I handled myself. It targeted areas of the Republican core where the Boss was irrelevant. These were voters who would vote the Republican line but break their ticket if they were given a good reason. With limited resources and workers, this campaign had to be selective. There could be no advertising, no rallies, and no broad mailing. It had to be limited to particular targets both geographically and by voter segment. Nothing would be sent to Democrats. No printed matter would be sent broadcast to Republicans.

There were three significant episodes that indicated my ethical issue was having an impact. The first occurred at the annual dinner of the South Nassau Lawyers Association This was a lawyers' association in Nassau County that was established by a group of litigators who wanted something less formal than the older, stodgy Nassau County Bar Association. At their annual dinner, they invited candidates. In preparation for my appearance there, I prepared copies of my memorandum on the conflict between the Cross Endorsement Ban and the Canons of Judicial Ethics. My children placed these copies on the tables of the diners where they could read them prior to introduction of candidates. Presiding at the dais was a lower-tier party functionary, a lawyer named Joseph Soviero. He was regaling the audience with wit that sometimes was caustic. The candidates were not invited to speak. Sevier would call the name and add some comment. Anticipating a "Soviero" caustic comment, I had moved to a table in the front row facing the dais. When Soviero introduced me, he added, "If Donovan is so ethical, why didn't he tell the Republican committee that he would not sign the agreement before they nominated him?" He made the same mistake that the Boss and Judge Scileppi had made. He challenged me. I was angry. I stepped up to the dais and grabbed the microphone from Soviero. I then addressed the lawyers. Taken aback by that bold move, neither Soviero nor anyone else interrupted my short talk. I had the attention of that audience.

The second episode involved a group called "The Mercy League." The Mercy League was a group of women whose purpose was to aid Mercy Hospital, which was located in Rockville Centre, Nassau County. One member, Mary Sheehan, was the widow of "Chub" Sheehan, a friend of mine. After I had held a meeting of men at a Knights of Columbus Hall in Hicksville, Mary visited me. She astonished me by saying, "You made a big mistake! " When I asked what the mistake was, she said, "You forgot the women." At that, she volunteered to get a group of women to assist in the campaign. Mary got together a group of about fifty women. I gave them booklets listing the voters in the town of Oyster Bay with the party affiliation of each voter. They wrote letters to the voters. To minimize expense and maximize effect, all the letters were handwritten and sent to Republican registered voters in the four major communities, Syosset, Farmingdale, Bethpage, and Massapequa.

The third episode involved Judge Beatrice Burstein. I had deliberately avoided intruding on Democratic Party events. As a long-time active Republican Party worker for about ten years prior to my ascending the bench, I would not have anticipated a warm welcome at such an event. If that background were not enough of a handicap, I was now campaigning with a Conservative Party endorsement. That endorsement was anathema to a Democrat. Caution indicated that I avoid risking the ire of the diners at any Democratic Party gathering. You don't play with dynamite. I did not want to attract the attention of the Democrats.

One Sunday morning, after attending church, I pulled into a Hicksville shopping center to buy a Sunday paper. By coincidence, Judge Burstein arrived in the center at the same time. She was there to attend a Democratic breakfast. I greeted her and she asked, "Are you going to the breakfast?" I told her that I was not a Democrat and was not going to the breakfast. Judge Burstein grabbed me by the arm and said, "Come on!" I entered the restaurant hall with her and she led me to the dais. She then introduced me and explained my issue. At a Democratic gathering, you could have no better sponsor than Judge Burstein. She had always been a formidable candidate, a threat to the Republican Party, a public speaker in great demand, and a leader in the Democratic Party. This public endorsement before an audience of the party workers was invaluable. It came straight from one of the most charitable and influential persons in public life in Nassau County. It was inspired by her recognition of the ethics of her profession and my courage in taking on the challenge.

Perhaps it is worth a short digression to consider the importance of ethnicity in politics. Let's think Italian. Let's think Irish. We have heard the "melting pot" theory so many times that we, the general public, sometimes forget the "tribal theory." Politicians are not so blind. The mayor of New York City will march in every ethnic parade held in his city. However much we may dislike the bias and division that is inherent in the "tribal" theory, a politician will ignore it at his peril. All things being equal, many voters will vote for kinsmen, Italian for Italian, Irish for Irish, Jewish for Jewish, and so on. I had always been aware of the "tribes" and had strong ties to the two most important in Nassau County, namely the Irish and the Italians. Since I was Irish and my wife was Italian, I started with a good basic relation to both groups. My natural relationship with the Irish was nourished by my participation with the Ancient Order of Hibernians and the Police Emerald Society. I met with them. I marched with them. I spoke at their functions, and most important, I entertained them with Irish ballads.

At the time of my fight with the Boss, the majority of the Republicans in the town of Oyster Bay and the city of Glen Cove were Italian. That was one of the reasons the Boss selected Tese as his candidate. What the Boss did not know was that I had stronger ties to the Italians than did Tese. I was a charter member of the Columbus Lodge of the Sons of Italy. This was the home lodge of Angelo Roncallo, located in Massapequa and the biggest lodge in Nassau County. My early association with Angelo led to my membership in that lodge. Prior to the advent of Margiotta and Roncallo, men who were neither Irish nor Italian led the county of Nassau and the town of Oyster. There was the fear among the Republican leaders that if the Italians united, they would rule. The only lodges of the Sons of Italy were small lodges in the city of Glen Cove and the village of Port Washington. There were token Italian public officials, but they were not officers of Italian organizations. An attempt to form an Italian American club in Hicksville foundered, whether by accident or design. The Hicksville leader, Jerry Trotta, would have better knowledge of the disaster than I.

I had been instrumental in Angelo's obtaining his first political job. I was a Deputy county attorney and there were three new positions titled Assistant county attorney created in my office. At that time Michael Sullivan was town leader in Oyster Bay. He was a neighbor and friend of mine. He was the proxy for Leonard Hall and Henry Eisemann, who made the important decisions for my town. Hall spent most of his time in Washington, and Sullivan was a political novice. They were not "in the loop" when county patronage was being dispensed. Sullivan was unaware of the new jobs that opened in my office. Two of those jobs went quickly to other towns. I phoned Sullivan and told him about these jobs and said that there might be a young lawyer in his town who needed a job. He found such a lawyer. He was Angelo Roncallo. Angelo got the job and took his first step up the political ladder. Angelo and I became friends. Massapequa was one of the largest communities in the town of Oyster Bay. It was predominantly Italian and predominantly Republican, but it had no community organizations. Edwin Lynde, who was a deputy county attorney, had ruled it for years. I haven't the slightest idea of his genealogy but he had neither Irish nor Italian blood, and he had no connection with the grass roots in Massapequa. Massapequa was a political vacuum. The first movement in filling that vacuum was the creation of an Elks Lodge. As a member of the Elks Lodge in Hicksville, I participated in the festivities attendant upon the creation of the new lodge in Massapequa. Prominent among those forming the new lodge were Angelo and his friends. There were several hundred charter members in the new lodge and conservatively, I would estimate that more than 80 percent were Italian. Shortly after that, I attended a political dinner and my wife and I were seated at a table with Angelo. He told me of the formation of a new Lodge of Sons of Italy in Massapequa and said I could join because my wife was Italian. I accepted Angelo's invitation and became a charter member of the new lodge.

At the first meeting of the new lodge, I saw that the members were largely the same men who had formed the Elks Lodge. Massapequa was no longer a formless community. It had taken shape, and its character was Italian. That meeting opened as a public meeting and several Italians who were major Republican officials were present. Among those officials was Joseph Carlino. Carlino was then leader of the New York State Assembly. He was not a member of any lodge of the Sons of Italy. He was a token Italian who did not organize Italians. After some introductions and speeches, all nonmembers were asked to leave. Carlino knew me well. I had worked closely with him since I had handled the Nassau County legislative program. He passed me on his way out and stopped to ask what I was doing there. I answered, "Joe, did you forget my wife?" The Italians were organized. The Italians were on their way. Today they hold more than half of the major public positions in the town of Oyster Bay and hold the leader's positions in both the town and the county.

Returning to the role of Italians in my campaign, needless to say, I spent much time with them during my political and public life. As with the Irish, I met with them. I marched with them and—on one occasion—sang an Italian song, in Italian, in a duet with my wife. The Boss had his agents out there spreading a message designed to turn Italians against me, but I too had agents. One night I received a phone call from a court employee named Carlino. He was at an affair in the Sons of Italy lodge in Glen Cove. That lodge, one of the oldest lodges in Nassau, was of major importance in the community life of Glen Cove. Carlino told me that there were men there saying that I didn't like Italians. Apparently the Margiotta agents were conducting a whispering campaign in Italian circles. Since the majority of voters in the both the city of Glen Cove and town of Oyster Bay were Italian, it was important to stop that campaign.

I said to Carlino, "You know that I am a charter member of Sons of Italy in Massapequa. Most of the members had no choice to be Italian or not to be Italian, but I loved the Italians so much that I married one."

I am sure that Carlino got my response out. But I needed more help than that to turn Glen Cove. That help came from an unusual source.

An independent group called the Integrity Party had been formed in Glen Cove. Mrs. Tracy, a neophyte who had determined to enter the political arena, formed the group. She was running for mayor of the city. Mrs. Tracy called and asked if I wanted to join her ticket. I asked a friend who was a reporter for the paper *Newsday* whether he thought I should accept her offer.

He said that I should not accept the offer because it might detract from the dignity associated with a judicial office, and it might cost me votes. I did not follow his advice. I needed soldiers in Glen Cove and Mrs. Tracy's support would give me that. Mrs. Tracy and her family spread my literature around Glen Cove at shopping centers and other public places. Mrs. Tracy told me that a number of people took her literature but said they would not vote for her but they would vote for me. I ultimately picked up 1,288 votes on that line.

Everything came together on Election Day. The final scores were:
For District Court Judge:
Donovan:

| | |
|---|---|
| Democratic line: | 37,541 |
| Conservative line: | 17,852 |
| Integrity Party line: | <u>1,288</u> |
| Total: | 56,681 |

Tese:

| | |
|---|---|
| Republican: | 47,028 |

| | |
|---|---|
| Donovan victory margin: | 9,653 |

For Supervisor of town of Oyster Bay:

| | |
|---|---|
| Republican Burke: | 61,210 |
| Conservative Yevoli: | 13,497 |
| Democratic Gutheil: | 29,473 |

Rearranging the figures for ease of comparison, we have the following:

| | |
|---|---|
| Enrolled Republicans: | 76,635 |
| Burke Republican vote: | 61,210 |
| Tese Republican vote: | 47,028 |
| | |
| Enrolled Democrats: | 56,177 |
| Donovan Democratic vote: | 37,541 |
| Gutheil Democratic vote: | 29,473 |
| | |
| Enrolled Conservatives: | 3,371 |
| Donovan Conservative: | 17,852 |
| Yevoli Conservative: | 13,497 |
| | |
| Enrolled Independents: | 17,297 |

We can judge the success of my campaign strategy by analyzing these tables. We should first look at the head of the ticket. A strong candidate can pull a vote for candidates down the line. Burke, Republican candidate for supervisor, was the head of the Republican ticket. He was a popular incumbent. Gutheil was a political unknown, a run-of-the-mill Democratic candidate. Burke beat Gutheil two to one and his vote of 61,210 set a record for an off-year (local) election. We would expect that the "coat-tail" effect would have helped Tese, but the result shows Tese trailing Burke by fourteen thousand votes. Where did those fourteen thousand votes go? Tese did not hold his Republican core.

Comparing Gutheil and myself on the Democratic line, we see that I polled eight thousand more Democratic votes than Gutheil. It looks like I held my Democratic core. But for me to win, as I did, by ten thousand votes, I had to make up the deficit of about 9,500 votes between Tese on the Republican line and myself on the Democratic line and find an additional ten thousand elsewhere.

If I had gotten the entire Conservative enrolled vote of 3,371, I would have fallen short by 7,000 votes. There were 1,288 a votes for me on the Integrity line, but I was still short almost 6,000 votes. I made that up plus an additional 10,000. Where did I get those 16,000 votes? I would have had to get the whole Independent enrollment of 17,000 to make it. But most Independent voters do not vote in local elections. We need but look for the 14,000 Republican voters who voted for Burke but did not vote for Tese.

My plan of targeting Republican voters with the ethics issue worked.

# CHAPTER THREE

## *Climbing the Ladder*

This book is designed to give the reader an insider's view of how a political organization is structured and how it works. There are people, like Kennedys, Rockefellers, and Bushes, so wealthy that they do not have to work their way up from the bottom. At this point I will exclude them from my illustration. There are thousands who climb the ladder, advancing step by step up the structure, to achieve public office and become congressmen, senators, judges, department heads, and the like. When I entered public office in 1948, I knew nothing of the political organization. My entry was unorthodox, but I learned to be orthodox. Come with me as I learn about the political organization.

My family, as most Irish Americans, had been Democrats. They voted the Democratic line but had no knowledge of politics. Their party was like their religion. Either you were a Democrat or an outcast. There were people who did know politics and who profited from their knowledge, but the average voter followed blindly. During the Great Depression, I searched for, and would accept, any job at any salary. I knew that the Post Office took on temporary workers for the Christmas season. I would have liked to get one of those jobs but had no idea as to how I could get it. I happened to be speaking to a friend who knew more than I about how things worked. The friend told to see my pastor, Monsignor Belford, and get a letter from him. I saw Monsignor Belford. He gave me a letter to the postmaster, and the next day I had the job. Lesson one: the clergy have access to the power and can get favors.

In my search for work, I took and passed many civil service examinations. I would get a letter asking if I were interested in an appointment. I answered yes every time, but I never got a job. In the meantime, my older brother changed his registration from Democrat to Republican. Looking back from my later position, I could have rounded up over a hundred relatives who were Democrats and demanded help from the Democratic organization, but we were not that knowledgeable. While I may have been high on the list, I had no political support. The politicians worked a rule to get their people appointed even though down on the list. The law permitted the appointing officer a choice of any one of the top three on the list. The officer could keep picking number two or three and the one at the top of the list would never be appointed. Armed with this knowledge, I went to the Democratic local committeeman who lived on my block. He was unaware of the fact that I had followed my older brother into the Republican Party. He told me to go to the next Democratic Club meeting and see the assembly District Leader.

At that time I had received the usual letter asking if I would accept appointment as a messenger in the State Mortgage Commission. I followed the committeeman's advice. I went to the meeting and after the meeting, I got on a line waiting to see the leader. When I saw him, I told him my problem. He picked up the phone and spoke to someone. He then told me to go the office of Mortgage Commission the next Monday. I went there the next Monday and was immediately hired. Lesson two: Find out who the man is in your area. See him. Join the political club and attend meetings and attend club meetings. My next lesson was in Nassau County.

After an unprofitable association with some young lawyers in Brooklyn, I was unemployed and in debt. I had recently married and was living in my aunt's house in Brooklyn. My mother had recently moved into Floral Park, a village in Nassau County. She was listening to her radio one day and heard that there were two openings for lawyers in the county. One was for law secretary to a county judge and the other was for a deputy in the county attorney's Office. She called me and suggested that I look into them. I had lots of resumes, so I mailed one to the county judge and one to the county attorney. I had no expectation of a response, but I went along to please my mother. There was nothing for me in Brooklyn, so I thought it might be better to move to Nassau County. I moved in with my mother in Floral Park. It was a bit crowded there, so a few days later I moved into a cold-water flat in my brother's house in Elmont, another village in Nassau County. To my surprise, I received a letter from the county attorney, Marcus Christ. He invited in for an interview. The County judge followed the rules. Since I had no political sponsor and had earned no political credit, he ignored me. Marcus Christ was not following the rules.

This was an unorthodox approach by Christ, but he was a man of vision. He was impressed by the resume and at that time had a dire need for quality assistance. Marcus was no political novice. He knew the rules, and he also knew how to bend them. He was the leader of the Republican Committee of the town of North Hempstead. He was also a man of unquestionable integrity and a brilliant municipal lawyer. Christ's political superior was the county leader, J. Russell Sprague. Sprague was also the county executive. That office of the county executive was comparable to mayor of a large city.

I had been a registered Republican before moving to Nassau County, but I had no political background or experience. At that time Nassau County was a solid Republican stronghold. Republicans held all public offices. Fortunately, I had the first qualification for public office. I was a registered Republican. But more was needed. I had no credits. I did not belong to a Republican club. I had never made a donation to the Republican Party. I had never worked in a Republican campaign. All these things are necessary if you would seek a public office. Christ was well aware of the fact that he was departing from the customary procedure.

The first question that Christ put to me was, "Are you a registered Republican?" I later learned the he, as every other department head, had a list of the registered voters. Since I was a new resident, I was not in that book. When I told Christ that I was a registered Republican in Brooklyn, he asked if I could get some proof of that fact. I told him that I could, and I later sent him an affidavit of the Republican captain in my old Brooklyn neighborhood attesting to my Republican status. Christ then asked if I could keep a confidence. I replied that I had served in Army intelligence and was certified by an army investigation. He was satisfied with my background but said that he could not appoint me as a deputy because there were a number of well-connected Republican lawyers competing for that job. He said that there was an opening for the position of "secretary to the county attorney," but it only paid $4,800 a year. He asked if I could live on that. The answer was easy. I was living on less. The man who had held that job had not been an attorney. He had been a sort of errand boy for the county attorney. Christ said that if I were appointed to that job, I would do legal work. He added that he would give me the two most important cases in the office and if I won them, he would see that I got a substantial salary increase the following year. He said that he would have to speak to Sprague about it. Only later did I learn what Christ had to do to clear me for the job.

Since the former secretary had come from the village of Westbury, under the party rules, the job belonged to Westbury and his replacement had to come from that village. However, that village leader could waive the job and let it go elsewhere. Christ had gotten that waiver. The next problem was to clear the job with the leader of Floral Park because, under the party rules, if the job went to a resident of his village, he would be charged with that job and would probably have to yield on some other job if he agreed to my appointment. The leader of Floral Park was the county purchasing agent, and his office was on the floor below Christ's office. Little did I know that my moving from Floral Park to Elmont would upset the whole plan. There was now a new player to be approached, namely the leader of Elmont and a new town, town of Hempstead. To get that waiver was a little more difficult. I had to do a little work myself. Christ told me to see the committeeman from my neighborhood in Elmont.

It was now December 1948, and there was a blizzard burying Long Island under a foot and a half of snow. I waded on foot through the snow to the house of the committeeman. Although I was a newcomer and he did not know me, he was very courteous and told me where to find the Elmont leader and how to get there. Straightway I set off to see the leader. If memory serves me, his name was John Hilgendorf. I told him that I needed his approval for the job with Marcus Christ. He replied, "Anything for Marcus!" I was cleared, and the following Monday I started work in the office of the county attorney. But a political storm erupted in Elmont.

Mr. Christ had advised me to join the local Republican club, attend meetings, and become part of the organization. Shortly after starting work on my new job, I attended my first Elmont Republican Club meeting. I saw Bill Meisser, the Election Commissioner, there. Since he was the only person there whom I knew, I sat next to him. As soon as the meeting opened a man, who I later learned was a lawyer named Barbieri, rose and angrily complained that "a nonresident had been given a job." A discussion ensued and I realized that I was the nonresident. I thought of joining in the discussion but asked Meisser, a more experienced politician, for his advice. He told me to stay quiet. The storm abated when Barbieri moved to have the leader stripped of power to approve job applicants until he had referred them to the entire Elmont committee.

After the meeting, refreshments were served. As I partook of the refreshments, I was standing with my back to Barbieri. He was rehashing the entire story and told his listener that the appointee was "a short guy with a mustache." I was a short guy, but I never had a mustache. He did not recognize me, so I avoided a confrontation, but I realized that I had made some enemies and had better move out of Elmont as soon as possible. Lesson three: if you intend to enter the political world, you must consider where to locate yourself. Having learned my lesson, I asked Mr. Christ where I should locate myself. He told me he would speak to Mr. Sprague but that he would suggest somewhere in the middle of the island, where the area was growing. He came back to me and said that Sprague said I could live wherever I wanted. I bought a house in Hicksville where the farms were being bought and transformed into housing developments.

This strict party discipline is not required if your family is composed of billionaires. If your family contains billionaires and you would like to hold public office, just hire a professional political manager and put your money on the table. You can buy the job. It will help if you are willing to live in a state run by a political party that needs your money and does not have strong candidates seeking jobs. Consider:

John D. Rockefeller, senator from West Virginia,

Jon Corzine, governor of New Jersey,

Michael Bloomberg, mayor of New York City.

Consider Rockefeller. Why would a man born into one of the richest families in the United States move to a place as poor as West Virginia? John D. wants to attain national office. He can't get anywhere in New York. His brother Nelson is holding forth in that state. Who needs his money? John D. must pick a less-prosperous state with no major personality dominating the scene. West Virginia immediately comes to mind. It is wide open politically and close enough to New York and Washington so that he can live there and still be close to those sites of power. John D. moves to West Virginia. John D. becomes senator from West Virginia.

Now consider Jon Corzine. Jon was a banker by profession and moved up in that field until he became a partner in one of the most prodigious financial institutions in America, Goldman-Sachs. He did not have to move. He could finance campaigns in his home state of New Jersey. Jon becomes senator from New Jersey. Then Jon tires of that and decides that he would like to be governor of New Jersey. Jon states his wish and the better-qualified lieutenant governor, the leading candidate, steps aside and Jon is governor.

Lastly in this select group is Michael Bloomberg, mayor of New York City. Michael is a very able man. He built a great business empire. He has all the money he needs, and he would like to move into the public arena. He is a Democrat in New York, a predominately Democratic city with a host of big-time Democratic officials eager to advance. They don't need Mike's money. The Republican Party in New York is so outnumbered and the odds are so strongly against that party's fielding and electing a candidate that there are few contenders willing to make the fruitless attempt to win a mayoral race. Mike looked at the city's Republican organization. They had no New York standout candidate, and they can always use more money. Mike made a more difficult decision than the other two rich men. He wooed the Republicans and switched parties. It is a tribute to his daring and imagination that he pulled it off.

I might digress to go back to my basic political strategy: "Hold your core and pick off you adversary's core." Mike might have had a problem holding his core. As a former Democrat, Mike could expect trouble with these voters. Switching parties is always dangerous, but the Republicans had nowhere to go and they were basking in the afterglow of the Giuliani reign where the Republican Mayor Giuliani was still enjoying unprecedented popular acclaim. His core was secure. Mike had to attract Independents and Democrats. Mike knew the part that ethnicity plays in New York politics. A large segment of the Democratic Party in New York City is Jewish. Remember the "tribal theory." Mike was Jewish. Would Mike's people destroy him because he had become a Republican when he decided to be of public service? The election answered that question, and Mike did a great job for New York City.

Greater than these are the members of the dynasties. They need no advice from me. They do not have to work their way up any ladder. They already sit on the top of the ladder. People such as the Kennedys, the Bushes, and new arrivals, the Clintons, have two of the essentials necessary to attain national office: public image and an organization. We don't hear much about the source of the Kennedy money. When Jack came on the scene, the Kennedy family was not a dynasty. They worked their way up in the rough and ready political precincts of Boston. The manager and the moneymaker was the father, Joe Kennedy. He knew the leading figures in his church, in the national political arena, and yes, also in the major criminal organizations. He had been an international bootlegger when that illegal enterprise was a flourishing business. His son, Jack, did not become president because he was a young, charismatic candidate. Jack's father, Joe, was behind him with money and connections.

A family with a less seamy history is the Bush family. They are of the American aristocracy. Unlike the Kennedys, our Bush presidents , present and past, did not have to make money. They inherited it. They did not have to form an organization. That, too, they inherited. There have been some changes since I was a young man, but you can still find the children of these aristocratic families in the lecture halls of Yale University. Their world is a different world. It is a world of wealth, power, and influence. They start at the top. The Clintons' political careers took different courses. President Clinton had to work for his wealth and position. He started at the bottom. When his wife, Hillary, launched her political career, the Clintons had already achieved wealth and power. She started at the top. She could pick her spot. Hillary needed a national platform from which she could launch her campaign for president. The Senate would be ideal. This was easy. She had her pick of the fifty states. New York State would give her maximum exposure and she would be guaranteed election to the Senate. New York State is so heavily Democratic that it is difficult for a Democrat to lose that state. Let's leave those who start at the top of the ladder and consider those, like you and I, who must start at the bottom. It is possible for us to climb that ladder. President Truman did it. He started at the lowest rung of the ladder, and without wealth, patrician background, or personal organization, he reached the highest position in the nation (albeit a little luck helped him along).

Since my purpose is this book is designed to give the reader an insider's view of how a political organization is structured and how it works, I will exclude people like Kennedys, Rockefellers, and Bushes, so wealthy that they do not have to work their way up from the bottom. But, even billionaires will do better if they move up the political ladder. Two billionaires come to mind who had some interesting ideas, spent a lot of time and money but accomplished nothing, namely Ross Perot and Steven Forbes.

Ross Perot, one of the most successful businessmen of his time, organized an independent party and ran for president in 1992. In modern political history, it has never been possible for an independent party (i.e., a party other than the major parties, Republican and Democrat) to win a national election. If Ross had been as wise in politics as he was in business, he would have recognized this fact. I cannot think that he had any idea that he could be elected president. If his objective was to help defeat the Republican candidate, George Bush, he accomplished that. A review of the totals in that 1992 election indicates that Ross drew votes that might have gone to the Republican. To this day I cannot see why Ross would have wanted to help elect the Democrat, Clinton, whose views were at variance with those expressed by Ross.

Then we had Steven Forbes, son of the publisher of the financial magazine that bears his name. Steven had some interesting ideas on tax reform, but he went nowhere, wasting time and money in a futile quest for nomination by the Republican Party. Either Ross or Steven might have done better to follow the Kennedy pattern. They could have used their money to start from a lower rung on the ladder, congressman or senator. This would have given them a national platform from which they could have furthered their objectives. Neither of these eminent businessmen recognized the system. There are thousands with less money who climb that ladder, advancing step-by-step up through the structure to achieve public office. You will find them as congressmen, senators, judges, department heads, and the like. If you have such ambitions, you must begin where Harry began and where I began.

In my search for work, I took and passed many civil service examinations. I would get a letter asking if I were interested in an appointment. I answered yes every time, but I never got a job. In the meantime, my older brother changed his registration from Democrat to Republican. Looking back from my later position, I could have rounded up over a hundred relatives who were Democrats and demanded help from the Democratic organization, but we were not that knowledgeable. While I may have been high on the list, I had no political support. The politicians worked a rule to get their people appointed even though down on the list. There was a rule that gave the appointing officer a choice of any one of the top three on the list. The officer could keep picking number two or three and the one at the top of the list would never be appointed. Armed with this knowledge, I went to the Democratic local committeeman who lived on my block. He was unaware of the fact that I had followed my older brother into the Republican Party. He told me to go to the next Democratic Club meeting and see the assembly District Leader.

At that time I had received the usual letter asking if I would accept appointment as a messenger in the State Mortgage Commission. I followed the committeeman's advice. I went to the meeting and after the meeting, I got in a line waiting to see the leader. When I saw him, I told him my problem. He picked up the phone and spoke to someone. He then told me to go the office of Mortgage Commission the next Monday. I went there the next Monday and was immediately hired. Lesson two: Find out who the man is in your area and attend club meetings. If you will follow my initiation and progress, you will learn how to become a participant in your local organization. However I was just a beginner in the study of politics. My next lesson was in Nassau County.

After an unprofitable association with some young lawyers in Brooklyn, I was unemployed and in debt. I had recently married and was living in my aunt's house in Brooklyn. My mother had recently moved into Floral Park, a village in Nassau County. She was listening to her radio one day and heard that there were two openings for lawyers in the county. One was for law secretary to a county judge and the other was for a deputy in the county attorney's Office. She called me and suggested that I look into them. I had lots of resumes, so I mailed one to the county judge and one to the county attorney. I had no expectation of a response, but I went along to please my mother. There was nothing for me in Brooklyn, so I thought it might be better to move to Nassau County. I moved in with my mother in Floral Park. It was a bit crowded there, so a few days later I moved into a cold-water flat in my brother's house in Elmont another village in Nassau County. To my surprise, I received a letter from the county attorney, Marcus Christ. He invited in for an interview. The County judge followed the rules. Since I had no political sponsor and had earned no political credit, he ignored me. Marcus Christ was not following the rules.

This was an unorthodox approach by Christ, but he was a man of vision. He was impressed by the resume and at that time had a dire need for quality assistance. Marcus was no political novice. He knew the rules, and he also knew how to bend them. He was the leader of the Republican Committee of the town of North Hempstead. He was also a man of unquestionable integrity and a brilliant municipal lawyer. In one of those rare coincidences, a political novice sent a resume to the county attorney of Nassau County and got an invitation to an interview. Christ's political superior was the County Leader, J. Russell Sprague. Sprague was also the chief executive of the county. He held the office of county executive. The office of county executive was comparable to mayor of a large city.

I had been a registered Republican living in Brooklyn before moving to Nassau County, but I had no political background or experience. At that time Nassau County was a solid Republican stronghold. Republicans held all public offices I had the first qualification for public office. I was a registered Republican. But more was needed. I had no credits. I did not belong to a Republican club. I had never made a donation to the Republican Party. I had never worked in a Republican campaign. All these things are necessary if you would seek a public office. Christ was well aware of the fact that he was departing from the customary procedure.

The first question that Christ put to me was, "Are you a registered Republican?" I later learned the he, as every other department head, had a list of the registered voters. Since I was a new resident, I was not in that book. When I told Christ that I was a registered Republican in Brooklyn, he asked if I could get some proof of that fact. I told him that I could and I later sent him an affidavit of the Republican captain in my old Brooklyn neighborhood attesting to my Republican status. Christ then asked if I could keep a confidence. I replied that I had served in Army intelligence and was certified by an army investigation. He was satisfied with my background but said that he could not appoint me as a deputy because there were a number of well-connected Republican lawyers competing for that job. He said that there was an opening for the position of "secretary to the county attorney" but it only paid $4,800 a year. He asked if I could live on that. The answer was easy. I was living on less. The man who had held that job had not been an attorney. He had been a sort of errand boy for the county attorney. Christ said that if I were appointed to that job, I would do legal work. He added that he would give me the two most important cases in the office and if I won them, he would see that I got a substantial salary increase the following year. He left off telling me that he would have to speak to Sprague about it Only later did I learn what Christ had to do to clear me for the job.

Since the former secretary had come from the village of Westbury, under the party rules the job belonged to Westbury and his replacement had to come from that village. However, that village leader could waive the job and let it go elsewhere. Christ had got that waiver. The next problem was to clear the job with the leader of Floral Park because under the party rules he would be charged with that job and would probably have to yield on some other job if he agreed to my appointment. The leader of Floral Park was the county purchasing agent and his office was on the floor below Christ's office. Little did I know that my moving from Floral Park to Elmont would upset the whole plan. There was now a new player to be approached, namely the leader of Elmont. To get that waiver was a little more difficult. I had to do a little work myself. Christ told me to see the committeeman from my neighborhood in Elmont.

It was now December 1948, and there was blizzard on burying Long Island under a foot and a half of snow. I waded on foot through the snow to the house of the committeeman. Although I was a newcomer and he did not know me, he was very courteous and told me where to find the Elmont leader and how to get there.

Straightway I set off to see the leader. If memory serves me, his name was John Hilgendorf. I told him that I needed his approval for the job with Marcus Christ. He replied, "Anything for Marcus." I was cleared and the following Monday I started work in the office of the county attorney. But a political storm erupted in Elmont.

Mr. Christ had advised me to join the local Republican club, attend meetings, and become part of the organization. Shortly after starting work on my new job, I attended my first Elmont Republican Club meeting. I saw Bill Meisser, Election Commissioner, there. Since he was the only person there I knew, I sat next to him. As soon as the meeting opened, a man, who I later learned was a lawyer named Barbieri, rose and angrily complained that "a nonresident had been given a job." A discussion ensued and I realized that I was the nonresident. I thought of joining in the discussion but asked Meisser, a more experienced politician, for his advice. He told me to stay quiet. The storm abated when Barbieri moved to have the leader stripped of power to approve job applicants until he had referred them to the entire Elmont committee. After the meeting, refreshments were served. As I partook of the refreshments, I was standing with my back to Barbieri. He was rehashing the entire story and told his listener that the appointee was "a short guy with a mustache." I was a short guy, but I never had a mustache. He did not recognize me, so I avoided a confrontation, but I realized that I had made some enemies and had better move out of Elmont as soon as possible.

The relationship that I had established with the leader, Russel Sprague, grew out of mutual respect. He respected my legal expertise and independence and never tried to have me give him an "opinion of convenience" (i.e., an opinion tailored to fit his wish),and I respected his authority and his political skill. He wished to see me progress in the political arena and told me, "Frank, you can have anything you want, but you have to play leadership politics."

I answered, "Mr. Sprague, you know I can't do it."

During my years of service under the Sprague regime, there was never a case of "Sprague versus Donovan."

However, I pass along to you the sound advice of Sprague, "Play leadership politics." This does not mean that you must be corrupt, but it does mean that you try to avoid conflict with your political superior. I never challenged my local or town leaders and I would not have challenged the Boss, Magiotta, if he had not tried to have me violate my ethical obligations. My response to Sprague was not because I did not accept the limits of leadership politics. It was my distaste for the sacrifices that were required.

To be a political leader means giving up a great deal of time, being away from home for extended periods, and foregoing many of the pleasures that attach to a domestic, private life.

You must be prepared to accept party discipline. This requires giving up much of your freedom. The episode narrated in chapter one of this book was not my first encounter with party discipline. When I began work in the office of the county attorney, Judge Christ asked me to agree to stay for two years, and after that I would be free to seek another job and he would help me if he could. In a very short time, I took on and won every major case in the office. This was good and this was bad. As my reputation grew, opportunities were presented, but I found that I was not free to accept them. I had become indispensable and the county executive who had succeeded Sprague, namely Holly Patterson, controlled my political life. My deal with Marcus Christ was no longer in effect. I first learned of this when Judge Christ was nominated for judge of the Supreme Court of New York State. Such a judge can select a lawyer as his law secretary. I was Judge Christ's first choice. The salary was a little higher than I was receiving as a deputy county attorney, and the work was to my liking. I would review cases, research the law, and prepare opinions for the judge. But this was not to be.

Judge Christ was scheduled to speak at my club in Hicksville. He called and asked me to get there early, as he wanted to speak to me. We met and he said he had to withdraw my name because Holly Patterson had said he needed me in the county attorney's office. I was in no position to challenge Patterson since Christ would not have supported me.

In the county attorney's office, my work was not restricted to one or two departments as the case with other deputies. My basic assignments were all matters dealing with taxation and finance, the Board of Elections, and managing the county's legislative program. But I had also become the go-to guy on any critical matter that arose no matter what department or agency was involved. In addition to managing the legislative program, I was also Nassau County's representative on the legislative committee of the New York County Officers Association. This was my introduction to the legislative process, the process that the public never sees. At that time, all local legislation (i.e., legislation affecting the municipalities) was screened through the State Comptroller's Office, rather than the Attorney General's Office. No one ever told me why that was so, but the attorney general was an elected official who could be from another party, whereas the state comptroller was appointed by the governor. Ergo, the latter would be of the same party as the governor and more reliable in seeing that the policy of the governor would be followed.

In departments, agencies, and committees, there is usually a key figure whom you would see if you had something to clear with that unit. In the state comptroller's office, that man had been a deputy named "Monty" Chamberlain. Monty retired from that office and became the executive secretary of the New York County Officer's Association. He was the key man on the Legislative Committee of the Association. For all practical purposes, Monty was the association. Monty was also well connected with the "upstate" leaders in the Republican Party. The Legislative Committee reviewed and made recommendations on all bills affecting municipalities. At the meetings, Monty would take a bill and explain it with his opinion. All present would endorse his opinion. I began to question Monty and occasionally would oppose him and carry the committee. Monty never got angry about my challenge. In fact, we developed mutual respect. Monty's principal contact was Governor Moore, former lieutenant governor and state comptroller under Governor Dewey. Moore, in turn, was a major leader in the upstate division of the party. One day Monty took me into his office and told me that Nelson Rockefeller was putting together a brain trust and that he, Monty, thought that they could use me. That job never materialized. Holly Patterson never spoke to me on either of those job opportunities. Patterson always kept matters secret.

The practice among the leaders in the Sprague regime was to meet every Monday morning in the office of the county executive to discuss policy matters. At those meetings during the legislative season, the legislative leaders, county supervisors, and town political leaders would review the proposals that I was preparing for introduction in the state legislature. During Sprague's regime, I was always present to explain the bills and make note of any decisions or recommendation that the group would make. Under the Patterson regime, I was never permitted to attend any of those meetings. I had begun to resent the fact that not only was I handling several times the load of any other deputy in the office and being paid the same salary, but I also drafted all bills and memoranda for our representatives in the state legislature. Every week I took an early-morning plane trip to Albany to brief our representatives on our bills, worked all day in Albany, returned home on a midnight plane, and reported for work the next morning. After years of working under these conditions, I was not happy and began to rebel.

I complained to my boss, County Attorney G. Burchard Smith, about my workload and asked for an increase of $2,500 a year to compensate me for the extra legislative work. Patterson, again without speaking to me, turned down that request. One Saturday morning following that incident, I had occasion to go to the office of Joseph Carlino in Long Beach on a couple of legislative matters. Joe had risen to majority leader in the State Assembly, and he was looking for an attorney. Joe asked me if I knew anyone I could recommend. Joe said he had to pick a non-Catholic because he had too many Catholics on his staff. I asked him if I could take the job. Joe said that I would be acceptable since everybody in Albany knew me. But again Patterson would have veto power. The issue was discussed at a meeting among Sprague, who was still chairman of the County Republican Committee, Patterson, and Carlino. I was not present nor did Patterson tell me of the meeting. I later learned that Sprague had strongly supported me and said that I had done so much for so many years that I should be permitted to make my own decision. Sprague carried the day, and I had escaped the Patterson veto. I then had a difficult decision. This was a golden opportunity, a boost in salary, and I could establish a private practice to supplement my salary. I liked Joe and would have loved to work with him. As much as I wanted to get out of the county attorney's office and increase my earnings, I was loath to accept a job that would keep me in Albany, away from family, all week for months on end. The choice was family or money. I chose family and stayed in the office of county attorney.

Finally everything came to a head. I was preparing legislation to create several new positions for judges in the Nassau County District Court. One of those jobs would be in the judicial district that embraced my town, the town of Oyster Bay. I met with Sprague to get his advice on how I should draft the legislation. I could draw it to be filled in the November election with the office to commence on January 1 of the next year, or I could draw it to take effect immediately with the interim vacancy to be filled by appointment by the county executive. Sprague said there was no final decision as to which way I should do it and that I should draw up two bills and hold them till the decision was made. He added that I might be interested in one of the jobs. Obviously Sprague and Patterson were at odds about who would be selected. Ultimately it was agreed to make the statute effective immediately. This put Patterson in control. Initially the town leader assigned the new judgeship to my village, Hicksville. This pitted me against Patterson in a bitter fight for the appointment. To appreciate the scope of the battle, we should consider the party rules.

The party rules provided that the town leader of the town where the job was situated would decide all patronage. The practice was to give the job to the town leader. If he did not want it, it was offered to one of the village leaders, called the executive committeeman, and if he did not want it, the job would go to one of the committeemen. There were two committeemen elected in each election district or neighborhood. Exceptions to this practice were rare. The first qualification for any job was committeeman. These were last on the preference list. If the job was a judgeship and the town or village leaders were not lawyers or did not want the job, it might pass down to a committeeman. I was not a committeeman.

Despite the fact that I may have been the attorney for the Nassau Republican Committee and handled litigation that had affected major public figures, I lacked the first political qualification for appointment to a judgeship. I was not a committeeman. I had been president of the Hicksville Republican Club, had assisted at the polls on election day, and worked on campaigns for years, but I was not a committeeman, and Hicksville had a number of committeemen who were lawyers.

One of the committeemen in my district was Michael Sullivan. Michael was a neighbor and friend of mine. He had been town leader and town attorney. After resigning from those positions, he had a flourishing law practice. He was not a candidate for the job, and I had no doubt of his support. The other committeeman in my district, Jack Herzog, was no problem. He was not a lawyer, and he and I had worked together in the district for years. This had become a battle to be fought on two fronts, namely the leadership level and the local or village level. Usually the committeemen will accept the decision of the executive committeeman. The executive committeeman in my village was Ernie Francke. Since I had his support, I did not anticipate any trouble at the local level, but Ernie had lost control of his group. Ernie told me that I would have to campaign among the fifty persons who comprised the Hicksville Committeemen's Council. Ernie added that I would now learn how many liars there were in the committee. I could expect some of them to promise their vote to every candidate. But what he either did not know or did not expect was that my friend and neighbor, Michael Sullivan, would oppose me. At a dinner, a friend and committeeman, Francis Anderson, took me aside and told me that I had better talk to Mike Sullivan about his support. I told Anderson that I should not have a problem with Mike. Nonetheless, I took his advice and went over to Mike. I asked him whether he would support me and—to my surprise—he said, "I will have to think about it because Bob Corcoran is my partner [a lawyer and committeeman] and Warren Doolittle is my friend [another lawyer and committeeman]." I knew then that he would not approve me, and I had three votes against me to begin with. There were two additional lawyer-committeemen who would oppose me: Philip Robinson and his ally, Leland Badler.

I knew that Patterson was quietly doing what he could to sink me. I also knew that Sprague was doing what he could for me. I also knew that my town leader, Tom Pynchon was generally allied with Sprague in leadership fights and that Patterson was allied with Congressman Leonard Hall, the de facto leader of my town who generally ruled through proxies. When Sullivan was town leader, he had held a proxy from the actual leader, Congressman Leonard Hall. It was unheard of to have all these major leaders involved in a fight over a minor local judgeship. But this was no ordinary contest for a local judgeship. The real fight was not about the judgeship. It was about Patterson trying to beat me and keep me under his thumb in the office of the county attorney but doing it without openly taking part.

Under the rules, this decision should have rested with the town leader, Pynchon. But Patterson was working, as he always did, avoiding confrontation and moving behind the scenes and skirting the rules. Patterson had a veto with the interim appointment, but he was not going to talk to me about it. The Patterson opposition came to me through an old friend, Forrest Corson, who had been publicity representative of the Nassau County Republican Committee and still functioned as the publicity officer for the party but held a position of deputy count executive. Publicity had come out describing the fight that I was having in the Committeemen's Council in Hicksville. Forrest called me into his office and said, "Frank, if Holly [Patterson] doesn't want you to have this job and you go after it, he will never forgive you."

I answered, "If Mr. Patterson calls me into his office and says that he wants me to turn this down and become his county attorney, I will say, 'Yes, Mr. Patterson.'"

He and I both knew that I had handled one county attorney who was so incompetent that he could not make decisions and another in his eighties who had my office set up next to his so that he could get me in a moment's notice. He also knew that, in official circles, I had gained a reputation as the best municipal lawyer in the state but I would never be county attorney under Patterson. He could not control me.

Under the party rules, neither Sprague nor Patterson could openly take sides. The decision, under the rules, was for the town of Oyster Bay and neither held any party office in that town. Sprague called me at home and said, "We can let word slip down that if you are not the candidate, the job will not go to Hicksville." I knew that this would be done through my town leader, Pynchon. Pynchon was in my corner, but he was loath to try to overrule the Hicksville committee. I told Sprague that I would fight it out in the Hicksville Committee. Sprague left off saying, "If you have the approval of your town, Patterson will have to have a lot of guts to turn you down." The issue came to a vote in the Hicksville Committee and I won by a vote of twenty-five to seventeen. But all was not over; Patterson still held the power of vetoing me and appointing someone else to fill the interim vacancy. A couple of days after the report of my victory in the Hicksville Committee, I was at a conference with Holly Patterson and General Podeyn, chairman of the Board of Assessors.

As we met, Podeyn said, "Congratulations," and extended his hand. Patterson sat stone-faced.

I said to Podeyn, "I cannot accept congratulations. It is now up to Mr. Patterson."

Mr. Patterson said nothing, and we went on with the business at hand. A day or two later, I was again in Patterson's office. This time it was with Norman Penny, town leader of the town of North Hempstead. Norm said, "Congratulations." I looked at Patterson. He smiled, extended his hand, and said, "Congratulations." This was it. The battle was over, and I was to be the judge.

This is an illustration of how the organization works. There are rules and the safe thing is to follow them. The leaders get prizes and distribute prizes. This is leadership politics. This is what Sprague said I must play. It is the way to move up the ladder. It is the route to high public office. The public was unaware of my battle, and except for those in the political arena, the public has little knowledge of what is required of those who aspire to public service. I record my battles to illustrate how the organization works, but I do not recommend that a political aspirant be a rebel. A rebel has little chance of advancing in the political world. I submitted to discipline unless I was asked to violate a moral or ethical principle or someone became so oppressive that I was moved to say *no*! I remind you that although I fought and defeated leaders, I was not alone. Every time that I fought a leader, other leaders assisted me.

# CHAPTER FOUR

## *Politics and the Courts*

The public has always had problems with the interplay between the courts and politics. Should judges be appointed or elected? Should judges have life terms? In the United States, we have both elected and appointed judges. We have judges with limited terms and judges with life terms. What is the ideal or best system? As with many things in a democracy, there is no ideal or best system. Partisan politics will have a hand in the selection whatever the method of selection or the term of the judge. When drafting the Constitution and designing the framework for our government, the founding fathers showed an awareness of the evils that government may visit on the people. The system of checks and balances was incorporated in their design in order to limit the power of public officials and public bodies. If any single branch of government was trusted more than the others, it was the judiciary. The Supreme Court of the United States was placed at the apex over every other office or agency of the government. Nine persons were given life terms and their decisions could not be overturned by any other official or agency. The founding fathers put their ultimate trust in a body that would be immune to partisan dictate or discipline and freed of any fear of economic loss that might be visited on them by any party, official, or agency adversely affected by their decisions.

No one disputes the fact that, given the limitations of their knowledge and experience, the founding fathers did a great job. They cannot be faulted for having failed to realize that setting a group of nine as the ultimate lawgivers they were really undermining the noble plan of a government, as Lincoln described it, "Government of the people, by the people." Did the founding fathers realize that in a body of nine we might expect division? Did they anticipate that a division of five to four would, in effect, permit one person to establish some of the most fundamental rules to bind us? Did they anticipate that issues such as abortion, gay marriage, religious freedom, and civil rights might be decided by a single person in a five to four situation or a six or seven majority? I suggest that you read some of the judges' opinions in cases by a divided court. Then read the Constitution to see what the founding fathers intended. You may be surprised to learn that the judges on both sides were using their own personal philosophy or political bias to decide the issue and guided by that personal bias, interpreting and applying (or inventing) a principle rooted in the "intention of the founding fathers." You will find the "intention of the founding fathers" being invoked to determine an issue that was beyond the imagination or the foresight of the founding fathers. If the founding fathers thought that they had taken politics out of the Supreme Court, they were wrong,

The interplay between politics and the Supreme Court during the second term of President George W. Bush was particularly sharp. Bush had won the presidency in a close race where he had strong support by what the media called the "radical right." For this group, the overriding issue was abortion. Their priority was to change the balance on the court to get a conservative balance of power. Opposed to that group was a group favoring a woman's "right to choose" known as "pro-choice." The former were primarily Republican and the latter primarily Democrat. In public statements and at hearings, the various senators avoided stating the issue clearly and questioning the candidates directly as to their position on that issue. Bush had two opportunities to select a judge. On the first choice he had a candidate whose conservative credentials were solid and who had a particularly impressive judicial record of superior legal scholarship. After a bitter partisan fight, he won approval by the Senate.

When the second vacancy occurred, Bush tried to sneak by with Harriet Miers, a woman who had worked with him in politics for many years. This was a personal choice. Her legal experience was primarily as managing attorney in a major law firm and service as counsel to Bush. She had no judicial experience and there was nothing to reveal her conservative credentials. Right out of the gate she was given a "kiss of death." Two powerful Democratic senators, Senator Schumer, senator from New York, one of the most virulent of the pro-choice group, and Senator Harry Reid, senate minority leader, had kind words for her. Senator Reid stated that, in earlier meetings with Bush, he (Reid) had discussed Miers as a possible choice. She immediately drew fire from the leading conservatives. The conservative attack was so strong that Bush withdrew her nomination. An objective analysis would lead one to conclude that this was a gross political mistake. Bush thought he had a candidate who would have no problem getting the approval of the Senate. She would have replaced the retiring woman, Judge Sandra O'Connor, and would have drawn support from those who had fought against his previous nominee such as women's groups and prominent Democrats. It is always dangerous for a politician to anger his base. In his desire to reward a friend, Bush had proposed a judge whose record was such that she could not have passed muster in the Republican-controlled Senate.

One of the most important, most discussed, most controversial, and most politically charged cases ever decided by the Supreme Court of the United States was Bush v. Gore. It was the case that directly influenced the outcome of the presidential contest between Al Gore and George Bush in the 2000 election. By a count of seven to two, the court found that a ballot recount being conducted in certain counties in the state of Florida was not using a consistent standard. A five to four majority further declared that there was insufficient time to establish standards for a new recount that would meet Florida's deadline for certifying electors. The net result was to permit Florida's Secretary of State to certify George Bush as the winner of Florida's electoral votes. This awarded Florida's 25 electoral votes to Bush to give Bush the majority of the Electoral College with 271 votes and he won the presidency.

Gore's lawyer was David Boies. Eminent legal scholars, including law professors from Harvard University, have debated the case. If I dare to intrude and offer my criticism, you may rightly question my credentials. The only time that the Boies firm and I clashed in court was in a case arising out of a land transaction in Suffolk County, New York. In that case the Boies firm represented a plaintiff who sought a judgment against a young lawyer named Thomas Carusona. The case never went to trial. It was so utterly devoid of merit that it was dismissed on a motion.

In addition to my other assignments in the office of the Nassau county attorney's office, I handled all proceedings involving the Board of Elections. Prior to my arrival in 1948, the local election law expert was G. Burchard Smith. Prior to his appointment as deputy county attorney, Smith was under contract with the county to handle all election matters. In 1948, a young man named Larsen filed a petition calling for a primary election in the town of Hempstead. At that time Hempstead had two supervisors. Their titles were "Presiding Supervisor" and "Supervisor." Larsen's petition named the office that he sought as "Supervisor at Large." There was a question as to whether or not the words "at Large" invalidated the petition. The issue was referred to Mr. Smith. His opinion was that the words "at Large" were mere surplus words to be disregarded and the petition was valid as a nominating petition for the position of "Supervisor." Mr. Sprague asked to have my opinion. I said there was an ambiguity since the words "at Large" might have been intended to differentiate the office sought from "Supervisor" and refer to "Presiding Supervisor." My opinion was accepted and the Board of Elections rejected the petition as invalid. Larsen took the case to court. I defended and won. There was no research nor extended study or discussion. It took about five minutes for me to arrive at my conclusion. Sprague liked it because his tactic was always to snuff out opposition as soon as it appeared. From then on the Board of Elections was my client. There were several routine cases until a case arose that involved a conflict between J. Russell Sprague, the Republican boss of Nassau County, and W. Kingsland Macy, the Republican boss of Suffolk County. Governor Dewey was also involved. When titans of this size are fighting, caution dictates that you avoid the conflict. The controversy arose from the publication of a letter that was designed to embarrass Governor Dewey, who was running for re-election in 1950. Macy, to whom it was written, had spread copies of it around, in hopes that it would embarrass Tom Dewey. It didn't; it was King Macy who got hurt.

On election night, Macy, running for his third term in the Congress, was beaten by 126 votes. A Democrat-Liberal, Ernest Greenwood, a retired schoolteacher, vanquished him. Macy angrily demanded a recount. It was the first time in thirty-six years that the district had failed to elect a Republican Congressman. Dewey himself carried the district by fifty-nine thousand votes. Something was amiss. The district straddled the line between Nassau and Suffolk counties. Macy had carried the part of the district in Suffolk County but was badly beaten in the Nassau County part of the district. Macy demanded a recount of the ballots, alleging illegal voting in Nassau County. If you would like to see how politics affects the judiciary, the case of Macy against Board of Elections is a good place to start. I don't know how Sprague sabotaged Macy's campaign in Nassau County, but he had to be the saboteur. No one else would have had the resources required to beat a Republican incumbent in a predominantly Republican county who was opposed by a Democratic neophyte.

In launching his legal attack, Macy retained the top counsel available. He joined the Board of Elections in both Nassau and Suffolk as respondents, but the allegations of illegal voting were confined to the voting in Nassau County. His attack began with an order to show cause returnable before a Supreme Court judge in Suffolk County. A war council was convened in the Nassau county attorney's office to map a defense. My first suggestion was to try to move the venue from Suffolk County to Nassau County. I did not want a "Macy" judge to sit on this case. How to do it? Who could amend the order to show cause? We needed a judge and an argument. Five or ten minutes of research revealed that only the presiding judge of the Appellate Division of the Supreme Court could amend the order and change the venue to Nassau County. We had to have an argument to persuade the judge. A statute required that any case against Nassau County or one of its agencies had to be brought in Nassau County. However, this case was brought against Suffolk County as well as Nassau. Therefore, that statute did not apply. With nothing else available, I argued that this case was essentially against the Nassau County Board of Elections because Macy made no complaint as to improper conduct in Suffolk County or by the Suffolk County Board of Elections. I surmise that there were phone calls that were not made known to me, but the venue was changed to Nassau County. We had the case out of the hands of any "Macy" judge, but no Nassau Republican judge wanted to touch it. The Republican judges were saved by having the order returnable before an elderly Democratic judge named Stoddard. There was little time for research because the case moved in a couple of days.

I was a new lawyer in Nassau with very little litigation experience, but my advantage over the high-powered lawyers retained by Macy was that I knew the election law. I always liked election cases. They move fast, putting a premium on imagination and movement. In New York, the lower court is the Supreme Court, the intermediate court is the Appellate Division, and the highest court is the Court of Appeals. A case like the Macy case can be in the Supreme Court on Monday, the Appellate Division on Wednesday, and the Court of Appeals on Friday. The Court of Appeals will often decide the appeal in the evening of the day the case is argued. There is little time for research or for preparing briefs. To be successful in that type of litigation, the lawyer must be able to think "on his feet." He must be quick to analyze, clear, and forceful in presenting his argument. The Macy case could have bogged down for months if we were not able to cut it off quickly. Our goal was to have the petition dismissed on its face. This would avoid the weeks that would have been devoted to hearing testimony and examining records.

The election practitioner will know a little principle that will take most attorneys by surprise. In law school, I was taught that the New York Supreme Court is a court of general jurisdiction and has jurisdiction over every type of case. Unless he has dealt with the election law, the New York lawyer will be unaware of the fact that the jurisdiction of the Supreme Court in election matters is limited to such jurisdiction as the legislature has given it. The summary jurisdiction of the Supreme Court in election matters is confined to about a half-dozen categories that are listed in the statute. If a case does not fit in one of the listed categories, there is no jurisdiction and the case will be dismissed. In addition to the summary jurisdiction in the election law, there is a broader jurisdiction, a remedy known as quo warranto. In the latter case the court may consider every aspect of the election and decide the title to the office, but such cases can only be brought by the state's Attorney General.

When we appeared in court on the Macy case, the chief court clerk, John Scherger, was standing in the well with some papers in his hand. As soon as I opened my motion to dismiss because the court had no jurisdiction, John began berating me. He cried out, "Don't you know that the Appellate Division has appointed a referee to hear this case!" A referee is usually appointed where there is a great deal of testimony to be taken. This saves judicial time. The referee will hear the testimony, write up conclusions with a recommendation, and send it back to the judge for his review. If the case went to a referee, this would take the judge off this "hot" case. I immediately told the judge that there was no need for a referee. There was no evidence to be heard, no facts to be determined, nothing for the court to do but dismiss the case because it had no jurisdiction, because the claim of illegal voting was not listed in the categories set forth in the statute for summary jurisdiction. Since it helps to say where the proper remedy lay, I added that the appropriate remedy was quo warranto to be brought by the State Attorney General. The case was dismissed and immediately appealed to the Appellate Division. In the couple of days that I had for preparing for my argument in the Appellate Division, I learned that I was right on the question of jurisdiction but wrong on the proper remedy. The remedy was not quo warranto in our courts. The Constitution provides that the Congress is judge of the election of its members. We had achieved our goal. Macy was gone from our courts to wither away in hearings before Congress. He had no success in Congress. He lost his seat in Congress and with it his leadership in the Republican Party.

When we look at Bush versus Gore from an election lawyer's point of view, we must plan our case with time in mind. There are fixed time limits in election proceedings in order to have everything completed in time for the candidates to be installed by January 1 when terms commence. The lawyer seeking to upset, or change, the results announced by the local election authority must consider the political bias of the court, agency, or official who will make a particular decision and plan his attack keeping in mind the strict time limits governing such proceedings. Herein lays the fatal flaw in the Gore attack on the results of the local election authorities. I suggest that you take a blank sheet of paper and mark on it from left to right as follows:

Local Election    Secretary of State    Florida Courts    U.S. Court
Board

Now place a toothpick or some other slender stick of wood under each column. You now have the stage upon which Gore v. Bush will be played out. The space between the columns and markers indicates the time between the proceedings in each of the agencies. If you move one of your little sticks to the left or right, you will increase one space and decrease another. The aggrieved party (Gore) likewise could affect the time intervals between the several stages of his proceedings. This is the job of the attorney. While the many officials, or judges, making decisions may not be corrupt or overtly political in their decisions, an experienced election litigator will consider that on a close question the official or judge may lean toward his political party. Now before you move your sticks, consider a couple of things that should affect whether you move a stick to the right or left:

1. You cannot appeal from a decision until the decision is made.
2. The Secretary of State is a Republican.
3. The Florida Court leans Democratic.
4. Your client is a Democrat.

Now we are ready to plan the Gore attack. Since the local board tallies will be reported to the Secretary of State, a Republican, and she will certify the final result, I would not expect her decision to favor Gore. My hope would be to win in court on an appeal from her decision. Since I can't appeal to the court until she makes a decision, I would not delay her decision. Now move the stick under "Secretary of State" to your left until it is quite close to the stick under "Local Election Board." Now look at what you have done. You have decreased the time between the decisions of "Local Election Board" and increased the time between that and "the Florida Courts." I have decreased the time in an area where I can't win and increased the time in an area where I have a good prospect of winning. What did Lawyer Boies do? He engaged in a protracted and fruitless effort to prevent the Secretary of State from certifying the election of the Bush slate of presidential electors. This was an area where he was subject to a Republican official where he had little chance of success.

Now move the stick that you had under "Secretary of State" to the left and close to the stick under "Florida Courts." Now what have you done? You have decreased the time between the decision of the Secretary of State and all subsequent proceedings. Boies had shortened the time he would have for the Florida Court, which leaned Democratic. The case was terminated when the United States Supreme Court, in a five to four decision, held that there was insufficient time to complete a recount of the votes. It is not my intention to bore you by discussing the merits or grounds of the decision. The case has been discussed ad nauseam among law professors, political commentators, and others All the Supreme Court judges had problems, which became moot with the holding that the recount could not go ahead because there was insufficient time. Why was there insufficient time? While Boies's conduct of the proceedings may not have been the sole cause of the insufficient time for a recount of the ballots, it was a substantial contributory factor. If he had correctly analyzed the case, he would not have spent such time and effort in holding up the certification by the Secretary of State. A comment by a Bush campaign attorney interviewed on television put the matter succinctly. He said:

So, look, the Gore people shouldn't have delayed the election contest deadline. We could have gotten this done [the recount] if they hadn't brought these lawsuits to move the certification [by the Secretary of State] back. They put themselves in this pickle and they really can't blame anyone else for the problem.

I was the attorney for the plaintiff in an action where judges at every level were intimately involved. The court employees in Nassau County had been on the payroll of Nassau County. There was a collective bargaining agreement between the employees' union and the county. Among other things, that contract provided for severance payments to be made to the court employees upon termination of their employment by the county. A new law was enacted that transferred the court employees from the county payroll to the state payroll. The statute eliminated the termination benefits of the contract and substituted provisions that substantially reduced the benefits provided by the contract. The Nassau County Comptroller sent claim forms to all court employees with instructions to fill out and sign the form in order to obtain payment of their termination benefits. As attorney for the Nassau County Uniformed Officers Association, I advised its members to refuse to use the forms provided by the Comptroller and that they should file claims on forms that I would provide. The Comptroller's forms claimed the reduced benefits provided by the new statute while my forms claimed the more liberal benefits provided by the collective bargaining agreement. When the county refused to pay on the claims I had provided, I commenced an action against the county.

The case was a "hot potato" for some judges. On one side were the court employees who worked with the judges on a daily basis and most of whom were from the same political party as the judges. On the other side were the county and the State Office of Court Administration. The facts were not in dispute, but I was asking the court to declare the new statute unconstitutional as an impairment of contract. I filed the action in the Supreme Court held in Nassau County (court of original jurisdiction). The case was assigned to Judge Tomson. Prior to his ascension to the bench, Judge Tomson had been Republican Leader in the village of Great Neck. This proved to be significant because New York Court of Appeals Judge Sol Wachler was also from the village of Great Neck. Judge Wachler had a local office in the same building as Judge Tomson. One would expect that the two might converse from time to time.

Judge Tomson called a conference to discuss the case. He notified the State Office of Court Administration to have their attorney attend. When I spoke with that attorney, he said he did not know why he was asked to attend. Since the facts were not in dispute, I could have asked the county to stipulate the facts and bypass the court of original jurisdiction by going directly to the Appellate Division. The purpose of the conference became quite clear when Judge Tomson suggested that I withdraw the action that was before him and begin a new action based on stipulated facts and submit it directly to the Appellate Division. This would get Judge Tomson "off the hook." He did not want to decide between the employees who surrounded him and the county and state administrators. I told the judge that I did not want to do all the paperwork over and would prefer to have a decision by him and than take that to the Appellate Division if I lost and if I won, my adversaries would have the work of initiating the appeal. It was obvious that Judge Tomson was not pleased with my approach, and I did not expect to win at that stage. You can imagine my surprise when Judge Tomson decided in our favor. I had more than a little suspicion that he may have talked to Judge Wachler about the case and Wachler influenced the decision.

The loser took an appeal to the Appellate Division and that court reversed Judge Tomson with a very strong opinion by Judge Shapiro. Needless to say, this case was the center of interest for all court personnel. At the argument, Appellate Division Judge Frank Gulotta, former District Attorney of Nassau County, sat at the bench although he was not assigned to hear the case. He and I had known each other for years. As I began my argument, I was immediately interrupted by Judge Shapiro, who asked a series of questions, all of which I answered, "Yes, your Honor."

He asked, "Do these employees have the same titles?"; "Do these employees have the same duties?"; and " Are these employees receiving the same salaries?"

It was apparent to me that Judge Shapiro had already made up his mind and he would decide against us. I could not quarrel with that. He had the right and duty to decide the case. What I resented was his rude interruption before I had a chance to utter one complete sentence of my argument. I had to treat him with respect, but I did not have to put up with his rough treatment. Before he could ask another question, I asked, "Your Honor, may I say a few words?

My emotion was apparent. I saw Judge Gulotta grin. He was probably glad to see someone challenge Judge Shapiro. Judge Shapiro was always a sharp questioner on oral argument but common courtesy requires that a judge allow an attorney to present his argument before being questioned on it. We lost in a unanimous decision. The opinion written by Shapiro was very sharp. It showed that he had little patience with our argument, an argument that was based on the clear language of the collective bargaining agreement and the county ordinances. He wrote that the clear language of the agreement must yield to the unexpressed intention of the legislature and the county (*Appellate Division Reports*, Volume 66, 2nd Ed., p. 131). The case is an interesting example of how judges sometimes "make law." Judge Shapiro saw our case as giving a "windfall" to the employees, and I must say that he was right. The question for every judge in this case was, "Can or must we permit this 'windfall' for the employees even though it is dictated by the clear language of the contract and county ordinances?" Ultimately Judge Shapiro was reversed by the Court of Appeals, but by a divided court, four in our favor, two dissenting, and one taking no part (Bennett v. Nassau County, Volume 17, New York Reports, 2nd ed., p. 535). Our victory in the Court of Appeals was due as much to luck and a change in the makeup of the court as it was to my "learned" brief and persuasive argument.

In this case, as in many cases, there are two issues to be addressed. On the one hand we have the "law." This is a study and presentation involving prior decisions, legal periodicals and treatises, and composition skills. On the other hand we have the effect of the decision. If both the academics are in my favor and the result is in the public interest or appeals to a layman's sense of justice, I love the case and am certain of victory. If, however, only one of those is in my favor and the other is against me, I know that I have a big problem. In the latter case, I am most interested in the particular judge's political, social, and moral makeup. In Bennett v. Nassau County, I had a strong academic position, but the public or taxpayer interest was against me. I had to convince the court that the statute that cut down the employees' termination benefits was an unconstitutional infringement on their vested contractual rights

Earlier I commented on the fact that Court of Appeals Judge Wachler and Supreme Court Judge Tomson had offices in the same building and lived in the same village. I surmised that our win before Tomson was an indication that Wachler might favor us. But then we had a bit of luck. I am always in a hurry. I don't like delay. The county was not prompt in prosecution of the action, and I was threatening to ask the court to penalize them for delay. However, their delay may have given us the big break that we needed. A new judge was elected to the Court of Appeals during the pendency of the action. It was Judge Meyer, who wrote the opinion for the Court of Appeals. Judge Meyer had been a Supreme Court judge in our county, and he was a friend of Judge Wachler. I spend time on this case because I am familiar with every aspect of it and because it dramatically illustrates what motivates judges. It tells us why we must be aware of the fact that judges, more than legislators, may shape the fundamental laws that we live by and the importance of evaluating the personality of those whom we choose to be our judges. In contrast to the Bennett case where I had the "law" on my side but public policy against, I will describe a case where the "law" was against me but public policy was in my favor.

A salesman took a client to dinner in a car that he had rented. After dinner, he asked his client to drive the car. The client was involved in an accident with another car while driving the car. A person in the other car brought suit to recover for the injury that he suffered in the accident. A controversy as to liability arose between two insurance carriers. One carrier covered the driver of the car and the other carrier covered the rental car company. Under New York law, if the driver of the car is operating the car with permission of the owner, the owner is liable. In that case the rental car company might be liable if the driver was driving with permission of the car rental company. The insurance carrier that covered the driver retained me.

To appreciate the way judges operate, you should know how the Appellate Division of the New York Supreme Court operated at that time. Our case was in the second department of the court. In that department there were about twenty judges who were assigned in panels of four for hearing appeals. My argument was brief. There was no discussion of law since the law favored my adversary. The rental contract was clear. Permission was given to the lessee, the salesman, and any employee or family member. The driver here was clearly not given permission of the owner-lessor to operate the car. I argued that the state of New York had a very firm policy of discouraging or prevention the operation of cars by persons whose ability to drive was impaired by the consumption of alcohol. In this instance, the lessee-salesman probably had a couple of drinks and felt that he should not drive, so he gave the keys to his dinner companion. I asked the court whether we should encourage drivers to act so cautiously. In the face of the clear language of the lease agreement, this was a pretty weak argument and I expected to lose this appeal. To my surprise, the panel of four decided in my favor. By coincidence, a couple of weeks later another case involving the identical issue came before a different panel of the court. My old mentor, Judge Christ, was on that panel. They came to a contrary conclusion, but in deference to their colleagues, they followed the decision in my case. On appeal, the Court of Appeals affirmed the decision in my case and that became the law of New York on that issue. I always felt that I stole that one, but it is of value when we are considering how judges decide cases.

Whatever your political philosophy may be or wherever you may fall in those convenient categories of liberal or conservative, you should be aware of the fact that judges hold the ultimate power and that, once appointed, the judges of the Supreme Court of the United States that establishes the law on the most important issues is subject to no one. If you wish to have a hand in the establishment of the law on these issues, you can only affect these judges by your vote in electing the president and members of the United States Senate. Personally, I am not happy with the system that permits one person on a divided court to establish law that will govern us in perpetuity. I am not unaware of the value of having judges who will brush aside the strict letter of the law to achieve some objective that promotes the public welfare.

Although the Nassau County District Court in which I presided is a local court of limited jurisdiction, I occasionally handed down decisions that were contrary to the opinion of my fellow judges where I found that the court administration was not serving the public interest. One of those cases involved an issue where I handed down two decisions that were inconsistent and the issue ultimately went to the Appellate Division. The New York Legislature enacted a statute that required judges to hold all persons charged with a violation of the drug laws for an examination as to addiction. This was designed for those charged with sale or possession of the heavy addictive drugs such as heroin, cocaine, and the like. Through error or oversight in the drafting of the new law, marijuana was not excluded from the operation of the statute.

The first time that I had experience with the statute, I was in the arraignment part of the court. That is the part where all new arrests appear. I knew nothing of the statute or the court's procedures until a teenager appeared before me with his mother.

He was charged with possession of marijuana. I beckoned the court clerk to approach and asked him how the other judges had been handling theses cases. He told me that the other judges were sending the young defendants to jail until they were examined. I was shocked by this procedure. The only cases that I knew of where misdemeanor defendants could be held without bail for examination were charges of prostitution. In such cases the procedure was sustained on the possibility of such women spreading venereal disease. I decided to break with the court and would not send the teenager to jail. I summoned the legal aid lawyer to come to the bench where I told him to object to the procedure. I released the boy in his mother's custody and ordered him to make an appointment to be examined. Arraignment court must move very quickly and for the most part it does not issue written opinions, but since I was challenging the chief judge of my court and not following the court procedures, I prepared and issued a written opinion. Although I was changing my court's procedure, I was not going contrary to the words of the statute. I required an examination. But I was not yet through with this statute.

Between the decisions refusing to hold the young defendants in jail for examination, I learned what was going on at the examinations. The judge would sign a lengthy document in quadruplicate. The defendant would visit the jail physician for examination. The doctor would have him roll up his sleeves and would examine his arms. He would then have the boy roll up his pants so that he could examine the boy's legs. I wondered what the doctor expected to find. If he was examining a heroin addict, he might look for needle marks, but marijuana use would leave no marks on the arms or legs. Of course the doctor was paid by the taxpayer for this ridiculous procedure. I decided to put an end to this nonsense. When I next presided at arraignment, again I had a defendant's attorney object to the ordering of an examination. Again I wrote a formal opinion to justify my decision. The neither the chief judge nor any associate judge of my court ever spoke to me about the issue. Since my decisions, although published in the selected court reports, were not binding on my colleagues, they did as they pleased.

The District Attorney never appealed from my decisions, so there the matter sat until a judge followed my second decision and his decision was appealed to the Appellate Division. The Appellate Division, by a three to one vote, affirmed the decision that the marijuana defendants should not be required to submit to examination and my old friend Judge Gulotta dissented with an opinion. His opinion repeated practically verbatim my first decision that required examination. He later told me how the case was decided. I saw the judge at a dinner and went up to his table to greet him. I told him that I had read his opinion in the marijuana case and thought it was well written. He then told me that there was a meeting of all the judges and they had my two opinions before them. He said a vote was taken and the majority adopted my second opinion. You may have guessed that I do not approve of such venturesome decision making by the Supreme Court of the United States, however, I do not object to a little constructive, independent thought by lower court judges. There is no appeal and no redress when the Supreme Court of the United States makes a decision, even if the decision is five to four, that permits one person to establish law. There is plenty of room for review and correction in the lower courts for change, if necessary, by act of the legislature. Even Congress cannot review or alter a decision of the Supreme Court of the United States.

Lest I go too far afield, my purpose in this introspective excursion is to give you an insight into how politics, the judge's personal philosophy, and the public welfare are all factors that affect the court decisions that may impact our lives. This business of judging is not all an objective search for the "intention of the founding fathers" or the "public welfare."

# CHAPTER FIVE

## *International Politics*

Let's jump to something bigger—international politics. This is an area where our lives and our families' lives are at stake and where we have little or no control. Whether it is the United Nations, our State Department, or some rogue nation, we find it difficult to analyze the problems or judge what should or should not be done. My purpose here is not to establish that there is no room in such problems for idealistic, equitable, or charitable motivations but it may help to apply here the same tests that we would use in analyzing a local, state, or national issue. Leaving aside a few public officials in any country who may sincerely try to bring about solutions that advance the welfare of all, the major actors are motivated primarily by two goals: power and money.

Let's start at the bottom and be both blunt and honest. With a few scarce exceptions, we, the voters, are all selfish. This is not evil. It is rooted our very nature. The primary aim of all creatures, animal or human, is self-preservation. The difference between us and the animal, and between each other, lies in the fact that we, or some of us, modify or control that selfishness by some moral principles. In analyzing an international problem, I suggest that we begin with identifying the self-interest of the nations involved and the self-interest of the leaders of such countries. This test is valid for monarchies, dictatorships, or democracies.

Let's go back to our history in attempting to formulate a mechanism for settling international disputes without resorting to war. Lofty, noble aims are thwarted by ignorance of the operative factors in such disputes. The first effort was the formation of the League of Nations. This effort was framed by the victors in World War I. It had no armed forces to enforce its resolutions but relied on forces to be supplied by the principal nations as required. It collapsed on its first test. The German dictator, Hitler, challenged the League with a public announcement that he had decided that Germany was going to reintroduce military conscription (compulsory enrollment) and build a new Army consisting of thirty-six divisions, totaling five hundred fifty thousand men. This was actually a flagrant violation of Part V of the Treaty of Versailles signed by Germany back in 1919 after its defeat in World War I. Breaking the Treaty was an affront to Germany's former World War I enemies, France and England. Everyone waited to see how they would respond to the news. But absolutely nothing happened. Because they did not see any damage to their self-interest, neither France nor England, the League members immediately affected, did nothing. We know how this led to the carnage of World War II. What did we learn from this blunder by the international compact? Apparently nothing. At the end of World War II we repeated the blunder, only on a grander scale. Building on the ruins of the League of Nations, we created the United Nations.

I never cease to be amazed at the utter stupidity of such attempts. A labor union leader would be unlikely to put the employer's bargaining agent on the board of directors of his union. If he went beyond that and gave the employer's bargaining agent a veto over board action, he would not last five minutes as leader. But that is exactly what our president and congress did as co-creators of the United Nations. We joined in putting our major adversary, Russia, on the governing council with veto power over its resolutions. We compounded this error by creating a bureaucracy to be controlled by a general assembly comprised of about 160 nations, some with populations fewer than the city of New York. Again there was a failure to accept, and make policy based on, the self-interest of the nations involved. When there were issues affecting its interests, the United States found no support in the United Nations. It had to resort to ad hoc coalitions such as NATO to block the threat of Communist Russia and leaving aside the validity of both actions, a coalition of nations in the first Iraq War, called "Desert Storm," and another coalition in the second Iraq War, called "Operation Iraqi Freedom."

At this writing there is still a problem between Cuba and the United States. Most people would attribute our differences to the fact that Cuba is a dictatorship and the United States is a democracy. We read and hear comments by political leaders, public officials, media "talking heads," and other experts feeding that erroneous proposition. It is false. After all, our country had no problem working with the Shah of Iran prior to the revolution that ousted him. We had no trouble supporting Latin American dictators when the rule was, "If he is anti-Communist, he can do no wrong!" At his point we still have friendly relations with Saudi Arabia, ruled by a royal family. As for democracies, Lebanon has a freely elected government dominated by an extremist Muslim organization called Hezbollah. Palestine has a freely elected government dominated by Muslim extremists. Iran has a freely elected government comprised of Muslim extremists. Democracy has little value in international politics.

Let's look a little beyond dictatorship versus democracy to see if there is something else that affects our relations with Cuba. Could self-interest or wealth be in the mix? Cuba's main crop is sugar, with tobacco a little behind. Who would want to stop our importing such products? Sugar is a big crop in our southern states. Tobacco is also raised in some of those states. Is it possible that senators, congressmen, congresswomen, and even governors and presidents would be looking for votes and campaign contributions from farmers who raise sugar beets and tobacco? Before the communist Castro came to power, Batista, a cruel and corrupt dictator, ran Cuba and the American mafia had free reign. Thousands of Cubans fled to the United States to escape the Castro rule. Most settled in Florida. They became citizens. They have votes. Those votes could be helpful in a contest for governor of Florida. They hate Castro and support a program to isolate him. The governor of Florida at this writing is Jeb Bush, brother of President George Bush. Could those votes be in the mix? That is not to say that freedom of religion, human rights, and other lofty motives have no place in the decisions of government, but we must always remember that the political leader and the public official are part of a political organization that is motivated by their need for money and votes.

We find a good example of how such motives dictated political decisions in a comparison of the divergent policies that followed in the two wars that we waged against Iraq. By coincidence, the first one was under George Bush senior as commander in chief and the second was under his son, George Bush junior as commander in chief. Both wars were against Saddam Hussein, the dictatorial ruler of Iraq. In analyzing any political issue, you must bear in mind that there are agreements and objectives that are known only to a few "insiders." However, you can sometimes figure out what agreements the leaders had or what objectives they had in mind.

In both the Iraq wars, the adversary was the same unscrupulous, cruel dictator, Saddam. In the first war, Bush senior vanquished Saddam's army in short order but stopped before invading Iraq and toppling the dictator. In the second war, Bush junior also vanquished Saddam's army in short order but went into the heart of the country and toppled the dictator. In the first war, Bush senior had the support of the neighboring Arab countries. In the second war, Bush junior went alone. After the first war, Iraq remained intact. After the second war, the country was divided with civil war between various sects, Muslim killing Muslim, and the majority of the victims were innocent civilians with no way to protect themselves. There were two radically different strategies with radically different results. Father was cautious and son was impetuous. Many experts asked why the father did not continue on to topple Saddam. If there were a confidential political agreement between Bush senior and his Arab supporters, he could not and did not reveal it. But by analyzing the position of the countries involved, we may be able to find the terms of the agreement and the reasons for the agreement.

Saddam's objective was to gain control of all of the oil in the area. His first attempt was an attack on Iran. On the heels of the revolution that toppled the Shah, Iran must have looked like a weak adversary. The Shah's army had been dissolved and the social, business, and government structure was in a shambles. What Saddam did not expect was the ferocious defense that Iran mounted with an apparent disregard for life with the enormous casualties that defense entailed. Saddam had to give up that attempt, but he did not give up his goal. He now turned to a softer adversary. His neighbor Kuwait was a nothing, no army, and no stubborn resistance. It was a cakewalk. From there he could walk into Saudi Arabia. With that he would control the world oil supply, and with that, he could control the world. He had no need for atom bombs. He could do the job in a few weeks. His only miscalculation was a failure to realize that the United States was not about to submit to his domination of the flow of oil, the lifeblood of our economy.

Bush senior was a competent politician. He knew that it would be helpful, and even necessary, to have the cooperation of the Arab nations surrounding Saddam. To get that cooperation, he had to talk to them and show that their self-interest demanded that Saddam be stopped. Let's examine the scene as Bush senior may have. Consider the self-interest of those involved. The United States needed bases from which we could launch our attack. Who had those bases? Bush needed Saudi Arabia. Why should Saudi Arabia give us those bases? What did the Saudis need? They were next on Saddam's list. They needed the protection of the United States. Self-interest joins these two, but the Saudi princes have another problem. At the bottom of Saudi society is a mass of Shii seeking to overthrow the rule of the princes. Shii are a majority in Iraq. Saddam is a Sunni Muslim and he has held the Shii in check. He is helpful to the Saudis in repressing the Shii. Turkey adjoins Iraq and had a problem with Kurds who dwelled in both Turkey and Iraq. These Kurds were a restive group, a headache to both Turkey and Iraq. For generations they had yearned to become an independent nation called Kurdistan, but Saddam had crushed that movement in Iraq. Turkey needed Saddam to keep the Kurds in check. Although Saddam's expansionist plans may have been a threat, the self interest of Bush's most important allies, Turkey and Saudi Arabia, dictated that Saddam should be de-fanged but not destroyed. If Bush senior agreed to his allies' demand to "de-fang but do not destroy," he would have been bound to honor that agreement, but he could not reveal the agreement. Can the mutual self-interest of the allies explain why Bush senior stopped short of toppling Saddam? In this analysis I claim no special knowledge. I know what you know. I read newspapers, watch television, and listen to the radio. I digest all that and do a little analysis using the same tools that you can use. Screen out the politicos and the commentators. Take the facts and apply common sense. You may come up with answers.

In the second Iraq war, we have a different commander-in-chief. It appears that Bush junior did not do much consultation with Iraq's neighbors, nor did he consider the rivalries or self-interests of the people of Iraq and the surrounding countries. He comes across as impetuous and arrogant. At this writing, Bush senior comes across as a success and Bush junior a failure. Instead of the democracy that he planned for the people of Iraq, he gave them a civil war that makes them risk their lives to go to work or to go shopping.

Lest you conclude that self-interest motivates other countries but the United States' actions are determined lofty, idealistic motives, I invite you to consider United States versus Iraq. During the long war between Iraq and Iran, the United States supported Iraq, an Iraq that was under the heel of the same Saddam whom we set out to destroy in "Operation Iraqi Freedom." As I write this, somehow an odor of oil seeps into the discussion.

# CHAPTER SIX

## *Politics and Business*

Thus far we have been discussing the operation of the political system in government. Let's change our focus to consider the interaction between the political organization and business. By laws and regulations, government has a powerful influence on business. As I began work in the office of the county attorney, I was immediately thrown into the area of the Public Service Commission's control of public utilities. The deputy attorney who regularly handled such matters was an elderly gentleman who appeared at rate hearings on bus or railroad applications. He sat through hearings and ordered copies of the minutes of the hearings. He did nothing else. His passive style came under criticism by a Republican committeeman. The complaint was that he had not represented the county. Although I had never handled any matter before the Public Service Commission, I was assigned to assist him.

After attending a couple of hearings with him, I realized that the function of the county attorney at such matters had nothing to do with the merits of the proceeding. In the ordinary application for a rate approval, before any public hearing is scheduled there will have been conferences between the attorneys for the utility and the Commission. They will have exchanged data and exhibits, and a tentative decision will have been agreed upon. The municipal attorney has a political role. He is there to represent the ratepayers. He should do two things. First, it should be apparent from the record of the proceedings that he was present and active. Next, he must ask a few questions but be careful to avoid being embarrassed by getting entangled with the complexities being discussed by the engineers, accountants, and other experts who are testifying. On one occasion I found a chance to do more than a perfunctory appearance.

The Long Island Lighting Company applied for a substantial increase in the price of gas it supplied for space heating. This was the time of the phenomenal population explosion that took place in Nassau County immediately following the end of World War II. The Lighting Company had been selling gas for space heaters at a bargain price and developers had been installing gas heat in thousands of the new homes that were being sold to returning veterans. There was a huge public outcry against the company, and from a political point of view, the county had to take a public position protecting the ratepayers. When the proceeding commenced, I did the usual, namely accompanying the senior deputy as his assistant. After the first day of hearings, I did a little research and found cases in states other than New York, where rate increases had been denied under comparable circumstances. In our case, Long Island Lighting had sold gas at cut-rate prices until it had a sufficient number of persons whose houses were equipped for gas heating. Then it sought an increase. This stratagem was like the loss leader used by retailers to get the customer into the store where he or she will purchase other items that are profitable. In short, the theory is: if you bring the loss on yourself by a marketing plan, the regulatory commission will not reward you with an increase in rates. I prepared a list of demands for information from the utility and presented it at the next hearing day. The attorney for the Lighting Company was surprised, but he made a quick move. He recognized that I was on a dangerous track. He knew from other hearings that the elderly lawyer was no problem. Addressing the hearing examiner. he complained, stating that the county could not have two lawyers. Since I was assisting the senior county lawyer, it was for him to come forth. He did nothing. I was silenced. The county's attorney did nothing, and the increase was granted. I then remembered a telephone conversation that had taken place between the county attorney and James Carpenter, attorney for the Lighting Company, before the hearings began. I did not hear what Mr. Carpenter, said but I have a distinct recollection of hearing the county attorney say, "Jim, we have to take a crack at you on this." The job was, "Hit the company but not too hard." I was learning.

At that time the population explosion had placed every public service, whether electricity, communication, or transportation, under stress. Shortly after the Lighting Company case, I replaced the elderly attorney and was the expert in all public service matters. The New York Telephone Company was about to apply for a change in their schedule of rates. I was called into the office of J. Russell Sprague to review the proposed schedule. He asked me to give him a report. The hamlet of Hicksville, where I lived, had been a farming area. I, along with my neighbors, had the telephone service known as a party line. With this type of service, as many as three or four homes were served by a single line. If you wanted to make a call and your neighbor was using his phone, you had to wait for the line to clear before you could place a call. I was familiar with that system because it was prevalent in an upstate area where I had worked as a farm hand during a couple of summers. I did not complain about it personally, but in my report I commented that an increase in rates where such outmoded service was prevalent was unfair. A few days after I gave my report to Mr. Sprague, my party line service became an individual, private line. I had not talked to anyone, and I assumed that the change was part of a change that was made in the whole neighborhood. It was only some time later that I learned what had been done. There was a problem with my service and the repairman had difficulty finding my line. Obviously the telephone company had made a special connection for my benefit in order to avoid any problem with me.

Zoning is a particularly sensitive area where government and business interact. In many communities real estate developers are major political contributors. Zoning and building regulations can stifle the expansion that feeds the developer. The law places a wide range of discretion under the control of local boards and legislatures. Lot size, type of activity, nature of construction, and the like are all under local control. Local control means a political organization holding power in the particular municipality.

Much of what goes on is behind the scenes. It escapes public notice. That is not to say that the profits of developers are always the result of corruption, but the developer must have the cooperation of the local political party. I could give many examples but will restrict myself to two situations close to home, New York City and Hicksville. If you have ever resided or done business in New York City, or driven through the city on your way to some other destination, you know what a mess it is: too much traffic, no place to park, overcrowded subways. How did this happen? Look for the developers!

If you are to build anything, you need a place to build it. You will seek and buy vacant land. But what if there is no vacant land to be bought? The developers and builders faced that problem years ago in New York City. They found an answer. If you can't build out, then you build up. What do you need, other than money, to build up? You need changes in local laws and regulations from those who control the height and construction of buildings and the required open space and other surroundings for the building. Who are these people? The local politicians! How do you get their support? You give them money! Even today we see huge buildings being constructed in the dense area of the city. This process of ever-taller buildings was denounced by technical historian Lewis Mumford in his book *The Pentagon of Power (Harvest/HBJ Book, 1997),* where he speaks of the Twin Towers as "an example of the purposeless gigantism and technological exhibitionism that are now eviscerating the living tissue of every great city."

The criticism of Mumford was dramatically borne out by the destruction of the Twin Towers on September 11, 2001. The Twin Towers, or World Trade Center, consisted of two buildings soaring above the city to a height of 1,731 feet. It consisted of 110 floors and on a given day would house fifty thousand workers and welcome two hundred thousand visitors. To make room for its construction, thirteen square blocks of low-rise buildings, some of which predated the U. S. Civil War, were destroyed. You might now ask, "Where were the politics and money in this scenario?" The original idea of building the project is credited to David Rockefeller and was vigorously supported by his brother Nelson Rockefeller, then governor of New York State. If we looked for a zenith in both money and politics, it would be the Rockefeller family. For another instance of the joinder of politics and money in New York City, we can hardly overlook the real estate tycoon and television celebrity Donald Trump. A short bit of research will show that the Donald covers all bases. He has been a substantial contributor to both Democrat and Republican parties.

We can leave the big city and go to my hometown, Hicksville. Prior to World War II, Hicksville had been a quiet farming community with lots of open, flat land generally zoned for residence. Farmers who, with hard work, managed to earn enough to support their families in modest style owned substantial tracts. A local citizen with better than average foresight bought up most of the land on the corners in the center of town. Today there is a thriving shopping area at the intersection of two of the major roads in town with a value of many millions. The tract on which that shopping center stands was originally zoned for residence. While still zoned for residence, that sagacious local resident bought it for modest sum. After the purchase, the zoning was changed from residential to business and its value zoomed. While the buyer made an enormous profit, there was nothing improper about the change of zone. Somewhere in the early 1950s, a fellow employee told me that all the politicians were buying stock in Roosevelt Field, presently home to one of the largest shopping malls in New York State, but then a vast empty lot zoned for residence. I did not have much to invest but I scraped up a few hundred dollars and bough some shares at five dollars per share. A few weeks later the zoning was changed to commercial, and the company declared a dividend of five hundred dollars. I had my purchase money back and still owned my stock. You can imagine the profit made by the "politicians." In most of such cases, the property was properly suited for business use. They are is cited here merely to show how zoning and building restrictions can affect the value of land and how developers can profit from advance knowledge and political influence to obtain, or expedite, the legislative changes.

As a deputy county attorney, I handled a matter that involved the most important business and largest employer in Nassau County, the Grumman Corporation. It was a project in which Grumman needed the cooperation of the Nassau County government. I cite this to show the necessity for business to maintain good relations with government. Grumman was a major supplier of aircraft for the United States government. The Grumman plant was surrounded by small homes in the hamlets of Hicksville and Bethpage. South Oyster Bay Road bordered the landing field and it crossed the Long Island Railroad at grade. Newer model planes to be constructed by Grumman required a longer runway. To lengthen the runway, Grumman would have to acquire part of the county road that bordered that runway. At that point the Long Island Railroad crossed the road at grade level. For the county to transfer the necessary land to Grumman required that the railroad crossing be relocated. The problem was compounded by the fact that New York State had established a policy that forbade construction of new railroad crossings at grade level. The project would require that the existing crossing be moved and replaced by a new crossing at grade. I first learned of the project when I was called into a conference with the county executive, Russell Sprague, the county attorney, Marcus Christ, and Grumman's attorney, Charles Kingsley. This project was without precedent and the legal work to get the necessary approvals was a bit complex.

The project would have to be considered in two separate jurisdictions. The first proceeding would be before the County Board of Supervisors who would conduct a hearing and make a determination as to the necessity of the new road. The parties to that proceeding would be the county of Nassau and the Long Island Railroad. The decision of the Board could be appealed to the Appellate Division of the Supreme Court. The second proceeding would be before the Public Service Commission. The Commission would determine the method of construction of the proposed new railroad crossing. At that meeting it did not appear that I would be assigned to any of the legal work. Sprague had a habit of calling me into such conferences on the chance that there might be something for me to examine. Since Mr. Kingsley was a more mature lawyer, much older than I, it was assumed that he would be the attorney in charge of the proceedings.

After that conference, I reviewed the law and concluded that Mr. Kingsley could not handle the matter. Grumman was the one who had the greatest stake in the project but it was not a party to the proceedings. He could not act as attorney for the county. That was the job of the county attorney. The county attorney, my boss, was not a litigator and did not want to handle the case. That meant that I, a neophyte, would be the attorney handling the case for the county. The county attorney and I convened with the county executive to advise him of the situation. I had only been on the job for a couple of months and had not been tested in any such matter. The choice was for me to handle the case or assign an older, more mature deputy. The shock of this announcement showed on Sprague's face. He hesitated for a moment and then gambled on me.

This should not have been a contentious matter, but there had been a change in the control of the railroad. It had gone into bankruptcy and was in the control of trustees. To our astonishment, the trustees opposed the project. There seemed to be no reason for the opposition. Sprague and Grumman had agreed that Grumman would bear all the costs of the project, even to the extent of reimbursing the county for the salaries paid to the county employees who worked on the project. There would be no cost to the taxpayers. The success of the project was vital to the thousands of Grumman employees. We were in the Korean War and Grumman had always been a major supplier to the government. Aside from the technical legal problem, this project was clearly in the public interest and without any cost to the taxpayers. I never could learn what motivated the trustees, but they were out to cause trouble. In matters such as this there are often hidden agendas and behind-the-scenes communications.

The political manager on this project was J. Russell Sprague, at that time perhaps the most important Republican leader in the United States. He had handled the negotiations with Grumman. In preparing the case, I could, and did, assume that our Board of Supervisors would approve the closing of the old section of the county road and authorize the construction of the new section.

At the hearing before the board, my job was to make out a record that would support the board's decision in the event that the Trustees of the Long Island Railroad appealed the board's decision to the Appellate Division. Grumman witnesses laid out the necessity of the runway extension to continue Grumman's work for the government and the impact on the local economy if Grumman had to cease its operations at the existing location. There would be tax losses to the municipalities, jobs lost by employees with the possibility of foreclosure on mortgages, and in short, an economic disaster for the community. There was no issue raised in regard to the public interest in proceeding with the project. The attorneys for the railroad surprised me with their attack. They raised an issue of public safety, urging that a plane might strike a train when taking off from the runway. Their principal witness testified to his qualifications and then gave his opinion that there was a real possibility of such a catastrophe. He testified as to his experience in designing airports and in flying. He had a pilot's license, which was one of the earliest ever granted. I listened carefully and heard nothing about his engineering qualifications or experience. I had what I needed. My cross examination was brief. I merely asked if he had any degrees in engineering and he answered no. I would make the case a battle of experts.

Grumman had given me a witness with the broadest education and experience as an engineer in airport design and maintenance. I reviewed the experience of my expert and had him testify to the existence of airports known to him that were bordered by homes. I asked if he had ever heard of a plane striking one of those houses while taking off from a runway. He answered no. I then asked, "If you had a stationary target and a moving target, which target would be easier to strike?" He gave the obvious answer. I summed it up to the board by calling attention to the fact that small houses bordered the existing Grumman plant and would continue to border the plant if this project never went forward. There had been no accident over the years that Grumman had been operating at the existing plant and the introduction of a moving train into the picture would create no greater hazard. The Board, as expected, approved the project. Also as expected, the railroad appealed to the Appellate Division of the Supreme Court. But unexpectedly, the railroad changed tactics. They dropped the safety issue and now charged that the project was not for a public use. It was solely for the benefit of a private corporation, Grumman.

That there was a special benefit to Grumman could not have been denied.

My response to this was two-fold. I first raised a technical defense, contending that, since the issue of public interest had not been raised at the hearing before the Board, the railroad was precluded from raising it, for the first time on appeal. I also pointed to the national interest, since the United States needed Grumman as a major supplier of warplanes. I also pointed out the losses to be incurred by the local municipalities if Grumman closed its doors and the dire consequences for the employees who would lose their livelihoods. Decision was reserved. Weeks went by as we waited for the decision Then I was alarmed to learn that Grumman had commenced construction of the project without waiting for the decision.

In the interim, Marcus Christ had been appointed a County Judge. I called him to tell him of this development and get his advice. He gave me advice that I should have gotten in law school. He said, "Frank, when what you are doing is in the public interest, the courts will be astute in finding ways to help you." A day or two later I was called to his office by Mr. Sprague. He told me that the decision would be in our favor, but it was being delayed because the judges had not been able to decide which of my two arguments would be accepted. When the decision finally came down, it was terse, with no legalistic discussion. The court said that the project was "in the community interest and the national interest." I suspect that, prior to my venting my alarm, Grumman had been informally assured of a favorable decision. The point to remember is that the interested parties have access to the public officials and that projects are regularly reviewed and approved in private conversation before any formal action is taken. This is true at every level of government from the village up to Washington. I must resist the temptation to expand on this point. Such a diversion would cloud what I hope to make a simple, but instructive, discussion of politics in action

# CHAPTER SEVEN

## *Your Role in the Process*

In a democracy, we must use our votes with care. We must study the issues and take positions that are in our self-interest and remember to moderate that self-interest with a degree of moral considerations. Perhaps I should pause here to say that if you find that I have either expressly or by implication shown a position on any issue that my purpose is not to argue for any position on any issue. I am trying to show the reader how the political system works. Sometimes the system produces good and sometimes the system produces evil, but at all times, it is a mechanism and you and I have the right and duty to see that the mechanism produces good. There are persons who understand how to use that mechanism and how to influence our use of the mechanism. They are like the athletic coach who is on the sidelines, but he sets strategy and tactics in the particular sport, be it baseball, basketball, or football. These political managers and public relations officers know and use certain established strategies and tactics to address the immediate situation. Partisan bias may be used by these tacticians to prevent you from seeing the facts. They are like the lawyers who represent a defendant where the facts establishing his guilt are overwhelming. His task is to prevent the jury from considering the facts. He knows that prejudice will blind the jury to the facts. I need not give you examples. Many of you followed the O. J. Simpson trial on television, a classic case where a murderer was found not guilty in spite of the evidence.

Why have I run you through what I learned after I entered the political world? I hope to help you to cut through the advertising "sound bites,", the slogans, and the other devices used in campaigns to divert your attention from an analysis of the facts. The system in which you have a vital role is not too nice but it is our system, and all who are involved in it are not selfish or dishonest. It reflects what we are as a people—good, bad or indifferent. We pick our leaders and they must represent our interests or they will not be elected. Perhaps it is time for some self-study. Do we want leaders who will strike out for the common good, or do we want leaders who will take care of our interests? Keep in mind my suggestion that the prime motivations of politicians are money and votes. Of the two, votes are the most important. Without votes, the politician is not elected, and if he is not elected, he is unlikely to make money. Let's try a little game where you are the candidate running for election to Congress.

It is post World War II and you are campaigning for Congress in a district that includes the Brooklyn Navy Yard. This is an old naval base and the most wasteful, unnecessary armed forces installation in the country. It employs many of the voters in your district and supports many small businesses in the vicinity. In the public interest, this installation should be closed down. Legislation has been proposed to close it down. You are asked to state your position on the issue. You know that the base is a waste of public funds. If you are a conscientious person ready to promote the national interest, you should vote to close it. But many of your constituents will suffer losses if the base is closed. You need their votes. Will you be honest and promote the national interest? I wouldn't bet on it. You are more likely to cater to your constituents and oppose the closing of the base.

Now let's continue with your candidacy for Congress but move you to a farming area in the Midwest. Your constituents are farmers. They receive farm subsidies. You know the farm subsidy program is wasteful. There are many who are demanding that Congress revise and cut back on the program. If you are a conscientious person ready to promote the national interest, you should vote for that revision. But many of your constituents will suffer losses if that program is cut back. You need their votes. Will you be honest and promote the national interest? I wouldn't bet on it. You are more likely to cater to your constituents and oppose any revision. We could repeat this scenario around the country.

Now you are elected to Congress. The congressman from Brooklyn is fighting against a majority of his colleagues to keep that wasteful base open. The congressman from that farm area is fighting against a majority of his colleagues to maintain those subsidies. What are such congressmen likely to do? Will they invite defeat by ignoring the selfish interests of their constituents and voting in the national interest? They are likely to join together. The Brooklyn congressmen will support both keeping that naval base open and continuing the subsidies and the farm district congressmen will support continuing the subsidies and keeping that wasteful naval base open. The two will talk to their colleagues who have similar problems in an effort to build a majority that will serve the selfish interests of their constituents, constituents that may be us and our friends and families.

If there be fault in what our representatives are doing, the fault is ours, the voters. They are representing us and serving our selfish interests. If we would like them to be different, we must be different. But can we curb our self-interest? This is how our democracy and our Congress work. It is often wasteful, but on occasion, our congressmen can show a bit of imagination and use the same procedure to accomplish something good. They did just that with the numerous wasteful and unnecessary military and naval bases around the country.

Our congressmen got together to do something that they recognized was in the public interest. Many Congressmen faced the dilemma that faced the congressman from Brooklyn. Individually they could not approve the closing of a base in their particular district. A commission was established and directed to set up a list of bases that should be closed. The report was reviewed and the result embodied in a single bill to be voted up or down without amendment. The Brooklyn congressman would not be asked to vote separately on the closing of his naval base, and he could tell his constituents that he could not vote against the bill that had the support of the overwhelming number of his colleagues and that he could not defeat the bill as a lone dissenter. The scheme was simple. The scheme worked.

As I write this, we are locked in an impossible struggle in Iraq. President Bush has been repeating, "Stay the course." The course has been wholesale slaughter as Muslims kill Muslims in an indiscriminate campaign of killing or maiming children, women, men seeking work, worshippers traveling to mosques, and groups congregating at shopping centers, public squares, or wherever. A sideline has Americans being killed daily. Critics are dismissed as cowards who want to cut and run. The president has received a stunning rebuke as his party, the Republicans, was soundly beaten in the previous election. As a voter or concerned citizen, how can you sift through the name calling and political gobbledygook spewed out on television. Without pretending to have any greater knowledge in such matters than the ordinary citizen and without any partisan or biased motive, but simply as an exercise in using the common sense with which we are all endowed, let's try to solve the riddle. Let's step back and analyze the problem in the light of a few observations.

To try to do the impossible is madness. By definition, the impossible cannot be done. If the hatred among the three segments in Iraq—Kurd,

Shiite, and Sunni—is so deep that, left to themselves, there will be civil war, so be it. To change such attitudes is beyond our power. Remember that the American model was tested by a civil war that was beyond anything to be envisioned in Iraq. If that is the fate of the Iraqis, we should step aside and let the Iraqis work it out among themselves.

Both establishment of a working democracy and the prevention of a possible civil war are impossible goals for the United States. If those goals are to be attained, the Iraqis must do it themselves with the United States protecting them from invasion by external forces.

Using such homely formulae, you can find your way through the advertising "sound bites," biased reporting, politicians' sales pitches, slogans, and invective to come to a reasonable conclusion on some otherwise difficult issues.

If you are to compete for public office you should prepare by selecting a political party. People have certain voting habits from which they may occasionally depart because of some overriding issue or special quality of candidate. Sorting out particular issues or candidates can be too tedious for many voters. Their solution is either to avoid the problem by not voting or voting a straight party line. In New York we use the old voting machines where you pull on a small lever over the name of the candidate. You can vote a straight ticket by merely running your finger along the line. The majority use that approach. That is where we get the base or core to which we may add others for a win. To be successful, the candidate will affiliate with a major party so that he may have a base or core vote. If, as in New York, there are two major parties, Democrat and Republican, and two minor parties, Liberal and Conservative, the ambitious candidate will have assured himself of getting a core vote by having allied himself with either of the two major parties. There is less competition, so it is easier to be nominated if you are a member of a minor party.

Most party line voters have an overall political philosophy that covers a number of issues but sometimes there may be a major issue that will override party loyalty and move them to vote for the candidate of the opposing part. When I was a child, the prohibition law was such an issue. It played well for candidates favoring its repeal. Today, abortion is such an issue. In the 2004 election, it gave George Bush the margin needed to defeat Gore in a close election. Voters seeking the overthrow of the case of Roe versus Wade realized that they needed a couple of conservative or strict construction judges on the Supreme Court. To get those appointments, they needed a president sharing their views. They got it by voting Republican. Bush appointed two conservatives, Roberts and Alito. Many of those voters knew that Bush was not the smartest kid on the block, but they accepted him in order to achieve a major objective.

Whatever approach you take in awarding your vote, the important thing is to use it. The nonvoter is not a good citizen.

# CHAPTER EIGHT

## *Who or What Controls Your Representative's Vote?*

Some years ago I happened to be at a conference where a new Republican Congressman, Steve Derounian, met with the Republican leaders. Steve had been a town councilman in the town of North Hempstead in my county. It was a bit unusual for such an unknown, low-level politician to be given such an important job. Steve got the job by default. The major leaders were all doing so well in the county that they did not want to go to Washington. Steve was a novice, but he knew that a congressman votes his own mind at his peril. Steve would follow the party line. He asked the county leader, "How will I know how to vote?" The leader gave Steve the name of the man in Washington who would tell him

On another occasion, I was directly involved in a situation where Long Island Congressman Stuyvesant Wainwright backed out of a program I had scheduled. That was back in the McCarthy era when Communism was a hot button. I was President of the Hicksville Republican Club and planned a debate on the issue, "Should Red China be admitted to the United Nations?"

Wainwright had agreed to be moderator. I had deliberately planned a controversial program because I knew it would draw a large audience. People love controversy. This would be a small community event, unlikely to draw much attention. I was surprised when I learned that my little debate had drawn the attention of the top party leadership. I was in trouble. Trouble with the leadership was the last thing I needed. I was employed by the county and served at the pleasure of the Republican county executive. I could have been fired without cause. I was vulnerable and it would have been unwise to defy the leadership. My town leader objected to the program and went directly to the county leader with a demand that the program be canceled. The Publicity Director for the county, a rabid anti-Communist, was furious. I was summoned to the office of the county leader, Russell Sprague. He suggested that I cancel the program. Sprague was one of the most capable leaders in the United States. He knew me well. He had hired me as an attorney for the county on my resume. I had handled every major case in the county and never lost one. He also knew that I feared no one. He listened quietly as I spoke. I said that I would be embarrassed if the program were canceled and that I would moderate the debate myself. I assured the leader that he would be pleased by the post-debate publicity where I would reinforce the Republican position barring China. He did not order me to cancel the program. This saved me from being defiant. He knew what I would do. The program went on. It drew a crowd. The publicity was great.

You may wonder: What is the purpose of all this narrative of leaders, political squabbles, and anecdotes? What does this have to do with your voting? I am trying to give you knowledge of how the political machine functions and the motivation and character of the people who control it. You should be aware of these things if you are to make prudent use of your vote. Thus far I have tried to keep this free of my personal bias or objectives that are, in substantial measure, contrary to popular trends.

Your vote is an important tool that you can use to affect the policy of your nation, state, or city. If we are to survive as a "government of the people, by the people, and for the people," we need knowledgeable, intelligent voters. We should study history and current events and examine ourselves. What are our goals? What will be best for our families, friends, and neighbors? What kind of a culture do we want? A democratic government will mirror its people. A Muslim democracy will display a Muslim character; an atheistic or pagan government will display a pagan character. Our elected representatives and our judges will mirror their constituents. Any student of constitutional law must see that questions now raised were never envisioned by the framers. Yet learned jurists seeing the vacuum not covered by the founding fathers will move into the vacuum and supply the void by inserting their own philosophy using the artifice, "If the founding fathers had considered this problem, this is what they would have said." They then establish supreme law from which there is no appeal and in a divided court, we have law established by one vote. These men hold their office for life. That single vote can lock us into a rule the will endure for a generation. It behooves us to take great care in our selections. We should have standards by which we judge issues and candidates.

In government, you have an executive such as a president, governor, or a mayor, but your closest representatives are a councilman in the city or state, a senator, and a congressman. A professional lobbyist will spend most of his time (and money) with these representatives. He will rely on them to get his message to the executive. You can become a lobbyist. With due respect to the legislator whose vote may be dictated by some moral or ethical issue, it is a rare legislator who may risk his job by voting in any manner that will anger his political "boss" or alienate a substantial number of his constituents. If you have an issue on which you would like to influence your representative, you can send him a letter. If there are others who share your view, have them send letters. If you are a member of an organization, have your organization adopt a resolution advocating your view and send it to your representative. If there is no such organization, form one. Remember the basic principle: politicians are motivated by money and votes. If his job is not jeopardized by a possible loss of votes, he will go for the money. He may not receive money directly, but the money will go to his political party and the party boss will steer the legislator's vote!

You should demand more of your representative. You should require that his conduct be moderated by a sense of morality. Many say that a candidate's personal life is immaterial. His public life alone should be considered. As I write this, we have Rudy Giuliani as a candidate for the presidency who was thrice married with a couple of extra-marital affairs thrown in. He is a leader in the pre-election polls. Apparently thousands are ready to entrust their lives and their family members' lives to a man who habitually violated his most sacred vows. What can we expect from such a man? One thing we know. He has no objection to the mass murder of infants. Is he what the founding fathers envisioned as a fit leader for our nation? Would he merit the approval of such as John Adams? Let's have a look.

"It is religion and morality alone which can establish the principles upon which freedom can securely stand. The only foundation of a free constitution is pure virtue" (Source: John Adams, *The Works of John Adams, Second President of the United States*, Charles Francis Adams, editor [Boston: Little, Brown, 1854], Vol. IX, p. 401, to Zabdiel Adams on June 21, 1776.).

"We have no government armed with power capable of contending with human passions unbridled by morality and religion. Avarice, ambition, revenge, or gallantry, would break the strongest cords of our Constitution as a whale goes through a net. Our Constitution was made only for a moral and religious people. It is wholly inadequate to the government of any other"

(John Adams, *The Works of John Adams*, ed. C. F. Adams, Boston: Little, Brown Co., 1851, 4:31).

Giuliani is certainly a champion of the principle of "separation of state and church," which he would like us to expand to separation of a candidate's morality from his fitness for public office. If we love our children and grandchildren, are we ready to bequeath to them a pagan democracy led by the most debased among us?

John Adams and Rudy Giuliani have a different view of government. It has taken over two thousand years and the sacrifice of millions of lives for us to advance from the Roman democracy built on paganism to the freedom that we have enjoyed in a democracy founded on religion and morality. From what the media feeds us, the rising crime rate, collapse of the family, the decay in sexual behavior, and the purge of religion and morality from every aspect of our lives, it appears that we are regressing to the pagan lifestyle that our forefathers fought so long and so hard to escape. In such a crisis, can we afford to have a pagan at the head of our democracy?

This is decision time. I have said about as much as I can or should say about the political system. It is neither good nor evil. It, like democracy, is a machine. It can and will produce both good and evil. Like most tools or machines whether it produces good or evil depends on the character and ability of those who control and operate it. You and I have a major role in what that machine produces. Years ago I read a simple line, a line defining our duty, "All that is required for evil to triumph is for good men (and women) to do nothing."

# CHAPTER NINE

## *You Are the Candidate*

Let's try a little game where you are the candidate. It is post World War II and you are campaigning for Congress in a district that includes the Brooklyn Navy Yard. This is an old naval base and it is the most wasteful, unnecessary armed forces installation in the country. It employs many of the voters in your district and supports many small businesses in the vicinity. In the public interest, this installation should be closed down. Legislation has been proposed to close it down. You are asked to state your position on the issue. You know that the base is a waste of public funds. If you are a conscientious person ready to promote the national interest, you should vote to close it. But many of your constituents will suffer losses if the base is closed. You need their votes. Will you be honest and promote the national interest? I wouldn't bet on it. You are more likely to cater to your constituents and oppose the closing of the base.

Now let's continue with your candidacy for Congress but move you to a farming area in the Midwest. Your constituents are farmers. They receive farm subsidies. You know the farm subsidy program is wasteful. There are many who are demanding that Congress revise and cut back on the program. If you are a conscientious person ready to promote the national interest, you should vote for that revision, but, many of your constituents will suffer losses if that program is cut back. You need their votes. Will you be honest and promote the national interest? I wouldn't bet on it. You are more likely to cater to your constituents and oppose any revision. We could repeat this scenario around the country.

Now you are elected to Congress. As the congressman from Brooklyn, you are fighting against a majority of your colleagues to keep that wasteful base open. The congressman from that farm area is fighting against a majority of his colleagues to maintain those subsidies. What are such congressmen likely to do? Will they invite defeat by ignoring the selfish interest of their constituents and voting in the national interest? They are likely to join together. The Brooklyn congressman will support both, keeping that naval base open and continuing the subsidies, and the farm district congressmen will support continuing the subsidies and keeping that wasteful naval base open. In an effort to build a majority that will serve the selfish interests of their constituents, the two will talk to their colleagues who have similar problems.

When they face a common problem, our congressmen can get together to do something that they recognize is in the public interest. The Brooklyn Navy Yard was not the only unnecessary, wasteful military base. There were many others throughout the country. Many congressmen faced the same problem. Individually they could not approve the closing of a base in their particular district. A commission was established and directed to set up a list of bases that should be closed. The report was reviewed and the result embodied in a single bill to be voted up or down without amendment. The Brooklyn congressman would not be asked to vote separately on the closing of his naval base, and he could tell his constituents that he could not vote against the bill that had the support of the overwhelming number of his colleagues. He would also tell them that he could not defeat the bill as a lone dissenter. The scheme was simple. The scheme worked.

Let's get back to your candidacy. Before you entered your quest for public office, you should have carefully considered your party affiliation. People have certain voting habits from which they may occasionally depart because of some overriding issue or special quality of a candidate, but generally they will vote the party line. Sorting out particular issues or candidates can be too tedious for many voters. Their solution is either to avoid the problem by not voting or voting a straight party line. In New York we use the old voting machines where you pull down a small lever over the name of the candidate. You can vote a straight ticket by merely running your finger along the line. The majority use that approach. That is where we get the base or core to which we may add others for a win. To be successful, the candidate will affiliate with a major party so that he may have a base or core vote. If, as in New York, there are two major parties, Democrat and Republican, and two minor parties, Liberal and Conservative, the ambitious candidate will have assured himself of getting a core vote by allying himself with either of the two major parties. The party-line voter will be his core.

Most party-line voters have an overall political philosophy that covers a number of issues, but sometimes there may be a major issue that will override party loyalty and move them to vote for the candidate of the opposing party. When I was a child, the prohibition law was such an issue. It played well for candidates favoring its repeal. Today abortion is such an issue. In the 2004 election, it gave George Bush the margin needed to defeat Gore in a close election. Voters seeking the overthrow of the case of Roe versus Wade realized they needed a couple of conservative or strict construction judges on the Supreme Court. To get those appointments, they needed a president sharing their views. They got it by voting Republican. Bush appointed two conservatives, Roberts and Alito.

Whatever approach you take in awarding your vote, the important thing is to use it. The nonvoter is not a good citizen. Your vote is an important tool you can use to affect the policy of your nation, state, or city. If we are to survive as a "government of the people, by the people, and for the people," we need knowledgeable, intelligent voters. We should study history and current events and examine our selves. What are our goals? What will be best for our families, friends, and neighbors? What kind of a culture do we want? A democratic government will mirror its people. A Muslim democracy will display a Muslim character. An atheistic or pagan government will display a pagan character. Our elected representatives and our judges will mirror their constituents. Any student of constitutional law must see that questions now raised were never envisioned by the framers. Yet learned jurists seeing the vacuum not covered by the founding fathers will move into the vacuum and supply the void by inserting their own philosophy using the artifice, "If the founding fathers had considered this problem, this is what they would have said." They then establish supreme law from which there is no appeal and in a divided court, we have law established by one vote. These men hold their office for life. That single vote can lock us into a rule that will endure for a generation. It behooves us to take great care in our selections. We should have standards by which we judge issues and candidates.

In government, you have an executive such as a president, governor, or a mayor, but your closest representatives are a councilman in the city, a senator and assemblyman in the state, and a senator and congressman in the nation. A professional lobbyist will spend most of his time (and money) with these representatives. He will rely on them to get his message to the executive. You can become a lobbyist. With due respect to the legislator whose vote may be dictated by some moral or ethical issue, it is a rare legislator who will risk his job by voting in any manner that will anger his political "boss" or alienate a substantial number of his constituents. If you have an issue on which you would like to influence your representative, you can send him a letter. If there are others who share your view, have them send letters. If you are a member of an organization, have your organization adopt a resolution advocating your view and send it to your representative. If there is no such organization, form one. Remember the basic principle: politicians are motivated by money and votes. If his job is not jeopardized by a possible loss of votes, he will go for the money. He may not receive money directly, but the money will go to his political party and the party boss will steer the legislator's vote!

You should demand more of your representative. You should require that his conduct be moderated by a sense of morality. Many say that a candidate's personal life is immaterial. His public life alone should be considered. As I write this, we have Rudy Giuliani as a candidate for the presidency who was thrice married with a couple of extra-marital affairs thrown in. He is a leader in the pre-election polls. Apparently thousands are ready to entrust their lives and their family members' lives to a man who habitually violated his most sacred vows. What can we expect from such a man? One thing we know: he has no objection to the mass murder of infants. Is he what the founding fathers envisioned as a fit leader for our nation? Would he merit the approval of leaders such as John Adams? Let's have a look.

"It is religion and morality alone which can establish the principles upon which freedom can securely stand. The only foundation of a free constitution is pure virtue." (Source: John Adams, *The Works of John Adams, Second President of the United States*, Charles Francis Adams, editor [Boston: Little, Brown, 1854] Vol. IX, p. 401, to Zabdiel Adams on June 21, 1776.)

"We have no government armed with power capable of contending with human passions unbridled by morality and religion. Avarice, ambition, revenge, or gallantry, would break the strongest cords of our Constitution as a whale goes through a net. Our Constitution was made only for a moral and religious people. It is wholly inadequate to the government of any other" (John Adams, *The Works of John Adams*, ed. C. F. Adams, Boston: Little, Brown Co., 1851, 4:31).

Giuliani is certainly a champion of the principle of "separation of state and church," which he would like us to expand to separation of a candidate's morality from his fitness for public office. If we love our children and grandchildren, are we ready to bequeath to them a pagan democracy led by the most debased among us?

John Adams and Rudy Giuliani have a different view of government. It has taken over two thousand years and the sacrifice of millions of lives for us to advance from the Roman democracy built on paganism to the freedom that we have enjoyed in a democracy founded on religion and morality. From what the media feeds us, the rising crime rate, the collapse of the family, the decay in sexual behavior, and the purge of religion and morality from every aspect of our lives, it appears that we are regressing to the pagan lifestyle that our forefathers fought so long and hard to escape. In such a crisis, can we afford to have a pagan at the head of our democracy?

This is decision time. I have said about as much as I can or should say about the political system. It is neither good nor evil. It, like democracy, is a machine. It can and will produce both good and evil. Like most tools or machines, whether it produces good or evil depends on the character and ability of those who control and operate it. You and I have a major role in what that machine produces. Years ago I read a simple line, a line defining our duty: "All that is required for evil to triumph is for good men (and women) to do nothing."

In earlier chapters, I limited my discussion to local politics and campaigns. National political campaigns are run by advertisers and require such huge staffs and so many millions of dollars that it may seem that we have no role to play at that level. Great issues will be decided in large part by officials whose careers began in the local arena. It is your vote or mine that helped them on their way. Be they president, senator, or congressman (or woman), they still need our vote. Your vote is valuable. Consider the millions of dollars that are spent on the campaigns to get your vote. Don't waste that vote. Study the issues. Take a position on the issues. Pick candidates and organizations that share your position on those issues.

# CHAPTER TEN

## *An Exercise in Political Analysis*

Let's take a current problem for an exercise. Let's analyze the controversial issue of Iraq. Iraq is an issue that involves the entire world and the lives of millions now and into the immeasurable future. If you have any doubt about the value or importance of your vote, consider that the issue will ultimately be decided by your vote and mine. Since at the time of this writing we are still embroiled in an effort to bring Iraq to a successful or acceptable conclusion, when you read this, the Iraq crisis may have been concluded. If that be so, this analysis may in retrospect appear to have been flawed. I take that risk. This is merely an exercise. I make no representation as to its wisdom. We will analyze the issue with nothing more than a little knowledge of history, commonly accepted facts, and a bit of common sense

Analysis is a thinking process. It requires concentration. At this point, I suggest that you put aside all distractions, things such as all the statements of politicians, and refuse to accept their terms of discussion. Your physical posture affects your analytical performance as well as your speaking performance. I find that I can analyze better while seated in a comfortable chair, and I speak better while standing and moving about. I attribute that to the fact that analysis is an internal process while speaking is an external process. I suggest that you sit back in a comfortable living room chair to begin this analysis. If you are comfortable, let's begin.

In this as in any discussion, we should agree on definitions, such as: what is a war? Speech writers, politicians, commentators, and "spin masters" have great skill in inventing phrases and slogans in which commonly used words are distorted to mislead us. Don't fall for such deception. Insist on the use of words with their common meanings. War should mean war; it is a word with both legal implications and connotations. We reject the use of phrases such as "War on Terrorism." Whatever the problem with terrorism and its control, the process is not war any more than the control or eradication of organized crime is a war. Such use of the word war is rhetoric rather than analysis..

In common parlance we understand war (other than a civil war) to be a conflict between nations fought by the armed forces of the respective nations. A war ends when the enemy's armed forces are defeated or surrender. That is the commonly understood meaning of a war. After a war has ended there may be a period of rehabilitation such as we had with the end of World War II. When President Bush appeared on a battleship and announced the "termination of hostilities," the war with Iraq was over. There remained a cleanup to restore order and install a new government with a functional infrastructure. We refuse to accept loose terms such as have been used by the president and our congressmen and other politicians to confuse us. In our analysis, war means war and the post-war operation is reconstruction. In defining the issue or question, we will exclude the controversy as to responsibility for the error in faulty intelligence as to whether Saddam had weapons of mass destruction. We will assume that President Bush acted in good faith and attacked Iraq to destroy weapons of mass destruction. We will further assume that his attack was a war despite the fact that Congress never declared war.

(*Aside:* If we may be permitted a short digression, we would like to reveal the spineless conduct of our Congress. In lieu of using its constitutional power to declare war, Congress passed a resolution that passed the buck to the president. If he did a good job they could share the credit. If he messed up—as he did—they could heap the blame on him.)

We had completed the reconstruction of both Germany and Japan with a minimum of civil disorder. Because of the cultural difference between us and the Japanese, it is a good parallel with Iraq, which also has a culture different from our own. Consider this quote from a commentary on the reconstruction of Japan under General Macarthur: "Macarthur's steadfast resolution to protect Emperor Hirohito—'through him it will be possible to maintain a completely orderly government'—probably ranks as the single most important decision of the occupation. Considering how well things went."

This was a simple act, but it catered to the long tradition that held up the Emperor almost as a deity. It showed a respect for the Japanese, and it went a long way in securing the cooperation of the people in the work of reconstruction This was in sharp contrast to what Bush did in Iraq. The lesson: Work with the local people. Restore and support the local leaders. This enabled the British to build and maintain the largest and most successful empire in modern history, with a minimum expenditure of their own manpower.

What did Bush do? Whom did he put in charge of the reconstruction of Iraq? He put in charge a man named Chalabi. Who was Chalabi? A ten-minute search on the Internet is enough to tell you who he is and why he was the worst choice to head up the reconstruction of Iraq. Chalabi was from a prominent banking family that had held prominent positions in the Iraqi government until Saddam Hussein's Baath Party took control in 1958. He was educated and taught in American universities. Except for a brief organizing attempt in 1990 in the Kurdish area of Iraq, he had not resided in Iraq since 1956. He was convicted in Jordan, in absentia, of a felony in connection with a bank of which he was chairman. He had connections with high=ranking officials in the U. S. government. His resume will be searched in vain for any connections among the local Iraqis or their leaders, such as tribal or religious leaders. His lack of support among the Iraqi people was dramatically established when his party failed to win a single seat in Parliament in the 2005 Iraqi election. Chalabi was Bush's mistake number one.

Bush should have had an overview on Iraq immediately after he announced the "end of hostilities." Anyone with a fundamental education in history and government should have been able to give it to him. Iraqis, as many Arabs, look to their sheiks or tribal leaders for direction. Iraq was a patched-up nation with three rival groups. The Kurds, Sunnis, and Shias separated into three areas. Saddam was a Sunni. During his dictatorship, the Sunnis had prospered and inflicted horrible torture on Kurds and Shias.

What was the Bush formula for reconstruction of this fractured nation? He was going to establish a democracy. To those with no knowledge of government, democracy is the key to all ills. Anyone with a modicum of knowledge of government and politics would know that in a "one man, one vote" democracy, representatives will mirror their constituents. We don't have to look far to see the fallacy in "democracy for all." Palestine is a democracy. Iran is a democracy. Lebanon is a democracy. Would you like to be living in one of those democracies?

This analysis requires no advanced study or expertise. It presumes a little knowledge of history, a little knowledge of classic battles, a little knowledge of human nature, and a good dose of common sense. How often have we heard the adage, "Don't bite off more than you can chew"? Have you ever applied that adage to classic military conflicts? Let's try a couple of modern or recent conflicts.

Hitler built a large, well-trained, and mechanized war machine. With lightning speed, he overran and swallowed up Austria, France, and a number of small nations. But Hitler was ambitious. He took on not one but two major nations, Russia and the United States. He tried chewing Russia, but it was more than he could swallow. He never recovered from that stupid error. His dream of world empire collapsed.

After the victory against Hitler, Soviet Russia continued on with its global campaign to defeat the United States. It chewed up a number of small nations around the world, but like Germany, its appetite exceeded its capacity. It could not swallow the United States. Another nation that bit off more than it could swallow. Another dream of world empire gone with the wind.

Japan versus the United States tells us the same story. As often happens, the Bible is not limited to religious themes. Sprinkled throughout that venerable tome we often find scraps of wisdom. Concerning the art of war, the apostle Luke quotes Jesus, "Or what king marching into battle would not first sit down and decide whether or not with ten thousand troops he can successfully oppose another king advancing on him with twenty thousand troops?" (Luke 14:31).

What is the lesson of history? The modern successes in Germany and Japan supplemented by the British success in building and maintaining its global empire tell us how to do it. The essence is:

1.   Work with the native leaders, culture, and organization.

2.   Keep your forces to a minimum and do not disperse them among the native people.

Bush set out to create a democracy with its "one man, one vote" mantra. He should have known better. Palestine is such a democracy. It is embroiled in a reign of civil war, terrorism, and violence that pits Muslim against Muslim and Muslim against Jew.

Iran is such a democracy with a government that pledges to exterminate the Jews and that is busy supporting an armed intervention in Iraq. Bush was faced with three very distinct groups divided by ethnic and religious heritage. They are in three separate areas outside of the capital city of Iraq—Kurds in the northeast, Sunnis in the northwest, and Shiites in the south. The Kurds had been living as an autonomous, semi-independent group under protection of the Unites States for several years before the fall of Saddam Hussein. All are Muslim. As in many Middle Eastern countries, their primary loyalty is to tribal and religious leaders. The Shiites have long been oppressed by the Sunnis under Saddam Hussein, and they are in the majority. Aside from the enmity among the three groups, there will be a problem in sharing the oil resources that are in the Kurd and Shiite areas. How would you address the problem?

Common sense and the lesson of history would suggest that we call a meeting of sheiks or tribal leaders and religious leaders. The Sunnis must be assured that they are not to be locked into a majority-controlled state dominated by Shiites. Shiites must be assured that the Sunni regime is not going to be restored. What did Bush do? He sent in his cadre headed by Chalabi and someone named Bremer with instructions to set up an election. This is in sharp contrast to what Truman did. Truman gave the job of reconstructing Japan to the larger-than-life General Macarthur and Germany to the legendary General Marshal. Error number one for the Bush-Cheney apparatus was that they never considered the three-province solution.

The three-province solution follows the pattern of the evolution of the United States. We began with sovereign states. For better or for worse, those states transferred much of their power and functions to the central government that we call the United States. But those states still retain their own courts, police, National Guard, and law-making power. In Iraq we found three separate groups with different religions and cultures with their own armed militias conveniently *living* in separate areas. They were and still are waging war among themselves aggravated by foreigners. They have been unable to compromise and work together. Since the Shia outnumber their Sunni adversaries, we cannot expect to force them into a "one man, one vote" government dominated by Shia. The three-province solution gives the Kurds, Shias, and Sunnis home rule with a delegation of a minimum number of broader functions to a central government. This was followed by error number two, the appointment of incompetent leadership charged with an unrealistic program as followed by steps that caused or exacerbated the chaos with its reign of crime and terror that ensued.

# CONCLUSION

This is decision time. I have said about as much as I can or should say about the political system. I hope it is helpful to those who aspire to public office or political leadership. I have spent much time addressing the problems of the voter. At election time the voter is presented with a mix of candidates. He is deluged with the statements of as many as ten candidates in what is called a debate. Questions will be posed to the candidates by a television commentator. They will have two or three minutes to answer. This is entertainment, not debate. How can the voter sort it out? My purpose is to give the voter some insight into what goes on in the halls of government screened by the utterances of "experts" on radio and television and to inspire the voter to study the issues on a daily basis. Newspapers, books, and magazines are much better than radio and television. They give us facts and arguments. Your common sense and analysis is often better than a congressman's speech that may have been written by someone else.

I write this last brief analysis with trepidation. I could be wrong. It is a personal prediction of the result in the 2008 presidential election applying the three factors I suggest to be used in any election. It is a test of my expertise. They are: X for the Democrat core; Y for the Republican core; and Z the swing or independent vote.

Remember the strategic plan. Hold your core, appeal to the independents, and steal from your adversary's core. To have a chance of winning, Clinton or Obama must hold the core, which includes blacks and Jews. They are major segments of the Democratic Party. Clinton is aware of this and tries to smooth over the animosity that has built up between them. She says, "If I become my party's candidate for the presidency, I would be honored to have Senator Obama as running mate for vice-president."

Obama says: "This is preposterous! I am a candidate for the presidency, not the vice-presidency!"

To hold the Democrat core, he should have said, "I am honored that Senator Clinton would select me as her running mate and if I should be selected as my party's candidate for the presidency, I can think of nobody more qualified than Senator Clinton to join with me as the vice-presidential candidate."

Obama has made a suicidal blunder. He has destroyed the chance of victory for both himself and Senator Clinton. The Democrat core is split, and barring some major blunder, Senator McCain will be our next president. This could have been avoided. A split of the Democratic core that is irreparable is apparent when we see the former Democratic candidate for vice president, Senator Lieberman, standing at the side of Senator McCain as they roam the country. Lieberman was rejected by the Democratic Party in Connecticut but won re-election as an Independent. He joined the Republican McCain on an issue affecting the existence of Israel. In the face of repeated threats by Muslims to destroy Israel, a strong case is built to suggest that Obama is a Muslim. It would be a rare Jew who would vote to have an American president with a Muslim bias. Obama has lost his core—and with it the election.

If Senator Clinton is the candidate, she will lose the core. Blacks (mostly Democrat) have been supporting Obama with estimates approximating 80 percent. He is a black Jack Kennedy. If he is rejected, they will not vote for Senator Clinton.

www.ingramcontent.com/pod-product-compliance
Lightning Source LLC
Chambersburg PA
CBHW030348290526
45785CB00004B/1653